My Journey to Appalachia

My Journey to Appalachia: A Year at the Folk School

Eleanor Lambert Wilson

Bright Mountain Books, Inc.
Fairview, North Carolina

Printed in the United States of America

ISBN: 0-914875-31-0

Front cover: Polaroid Image Transfer by Mary Jo Brezny
Back cover: Photograph by Mary Jo Brezny

Library of Congress Cataloging-in-Publication Data

Wilson, Eleanor Lambert, 1919-
  My journey to Appalachia : a year at the Folk School / Eleanor Lambert Wilson.
    p. cm
  ISBN 0-914875-31-0 (pbk.)
  1. Wilson, Eleanor Lambert, 1919– 2. Appalachian Region, Southern — Social life and customs. 3. Appalachian Region, Southern — Biography. 4. John C. Campbell Folk School. 5. Campbell, Olive D. (Olive Dame), 1882-1954. I. Title.

F217.A65.W55 2004
975.6'9042 — dc22
                                        2004009358

Dedication

To the many people of these mountains
whom I have known and loved . . .

"He has brought us by faith into this experience of God's grace, in which we now live. And so we boast of the hope we have of sharing God's glory! We also boast of our troubles because we know that trouble produces endurance, endurance brings God's approval, and His approval creates hope. This hope does not disappoint us, for God has poured out His love into our hearts by means of the Holy Spirit, who is God's gift to us."

—*Romans 5:2-5 Good News Translation of the Holy Bible*

Acknowledgments

To my family, Florence Atwood, John Wilson, Anne Harper, and Daniel Wilson, and to numerous friends, I give my thanks for their love, support, and assistance. I am grateful to Cynthia Bright at Bright Mountain Books, and to God, who brought my book to her attention. I am very thankful to my tireless editors, Dr. Benjamin Kennedy, Nancy Peacock, and Phyllis Baker.

My deep appreciation goes to the director of the John C. Campbell Folk School, Jan Davidson; retired director, Esther Manchester; and the staff of the school for their encouragement and enthusiasm. Thanks to writing teachers Nancy Simpson, Steven Harvey, Sharyn McCrumb, and to Jim and Margery Tucker, who taught me as much as I could learn about computers. A special thanks to Virginia Reynolds for creating the original watercolor map of the John C. Campbell Folk School on page vi.

I am thankful for my readers, my writers' group, my listeners at "Morning Song," Anne and Bill Wolf, Lissi Øland, and Turner Guidry, and all those friends who have said repeatedly, "Get it published. We want to read it!"

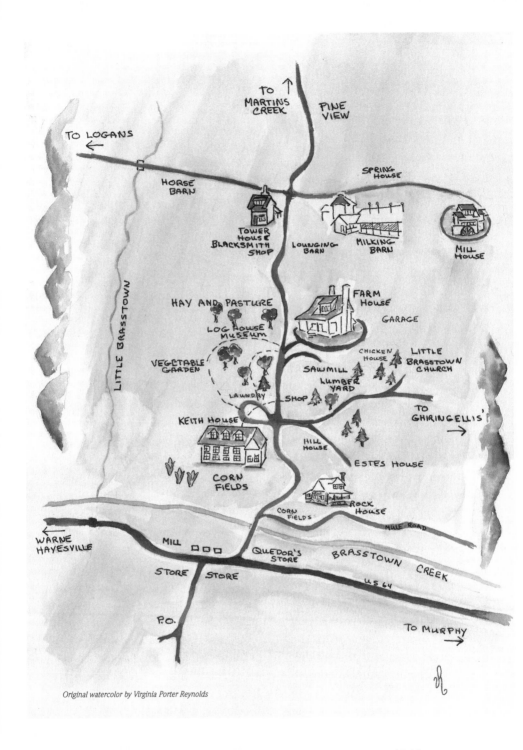

Original watercolor by Virginia Porter Reynolds

Map of John C. Campbell Folk School as it was in 1941

Contents

My Journey to Appalachia

Introduction

IN THE SOUTHWESTERN CORNER of North Carolina, the Great Smoky Mountains soften as they slope westward toward Tennessee and south into Georgia. The forests are green and streams abundant. In 1925, the small towns and farms were isolated. Transportation was difficult. Families were resourceful and independent, often self-educated.

In that year, Olive Dame Campbell founded the John C. Campbell Folk School, in memory of her husband. She chose the community of Brasstown, where a creek flowing down from Brasstown Bald, the highest mountain in Georgia, joins the Hiwassee River on its course to the Tennessee. Olive Campbell modeled the school after the Danish folk schools, formed to educate rural people in the art of becoming responsible citizens in a democratic society. The people here welcomed it.

In the eighty years since Olive Campbell and Marguerite Butler came to Brasstown, this community and the world have changed mightily. The area is no longer isolated, in spite of boasting that it is "one hundred miles from anywhere." The school that they planted with seeds of hope has grown into a center of creative life for people who come from everywhere. Many have stayed, drawn by a unique sense of belonging here.

The school was sixteen years old when I discovered it on my way around the world. This is the story of my impressions and memories of the year that changed my life long ago.

Choices

"It was . . . my senior year at Vassar."

IT WAS LATE WINTER of my senior year at Vassar College. The suite that I shared with three roommates was furnished with the castoffs we had collected during our four years together. Liz and Peg had pooled resources in their freshman year to buy a sagging cot that we all used as a couch at one time or another, in various dorms throughout our years together. Ann had contributed an overstuffed armchair with unruly springs, and I had collected a number of interesting pictures that graced the walls. The usual college furniture provided essentials. We were a gregarious group, and in our senior year we managed to secure the suite on the first floor of Main nearest to the post office and dining hall. At midmorning, our rooms provided a convenient gathering place for friends who had just been to the mailbox.

It was 1941, and the country was just emerging from the Great Depression. World peace and poverty were major social concerns. War was rampant in Europe and threatening in the Far East. There was widespread support for Great Britain, but many students marched in favor of peace. Debates about communism, socialism, and democracy were lively. Plans to relieve poverty and to restore land ravaged by poor conservation and eroded by dust storms filled student newspapers and stimulated midnight bull sessions. There was a sense of unrest and injustice in the world. As we dealt with the expectation of war, there was little readiness to make permanent decisions. The need to do something useful hung heavily on our shoulders; jobs were still hard to find. Everyone was asking everyone else, "What are you going to do next year?"

Graduate school and marriage were options for many. Most of us expected to have some sort of a career, perhaps in teaching, nursing, business, or politics. I couldn't afford graduate school. I needed a job, and I wanted to see parts of the world other than the Northeast. A cover on the *New Yorker* pictured the world across the Hudson River from New York as a vague wilderness. I wanted to disabuse myself from such provincialism, to broaden my life experience, and to write, but I had to support myself.

The sun slanted in through the long south window onto the floor, where Peg, my suite-mate, sat cross-legged amid notes for a senior course paper on the history of Asian art. The rays glinted off the edge of her white coffee cup, purloined from the dining hall that morning and refilled with her own brew from the battered aluminum percolator. The rich aroma of coffee mingled pleasantly with a pale overlay of Marlboro smoke.

She tapped her cigarette ashes into a saucer, overloaded with butts, and opened a long envelope carefully. A broad smile lighted her tanned face as she read. Then with one hand, she waved the letter triumphantly over her head. "I'm in," she crowed. "Harvard School of Architecture, here I come!" We cheered heartily and then turned to our own assortments of mail. Actually, we all had known Peg would make it and were not at all surprised.

Roused by the hubbub, Ann appeared sleepily in the doorway from the bedroom. Her hair was in large pink curlers, her blue satin housecoat wrapped loosely around her trim body. "Anything for me?" she asked in a voice husky from too little sleep after a long weekend at Yale. She paused and looked hopefully around the room. "I was expecting that invitation to Princeton," she said wistfully. We booed in mock envy.

"Nothing yet," I replied. Ann and I shared a post office box, and her mail was always more exciting than mine. I indicated her collection where I had placed it on the rumpled India print spread covering the sofa. She picked her way across the room and sank among the pillows to look it over.

About that time, Trish bustled in from the hallway. She clutched pages of typewritten material. Quickly she sat beside Peg on the threadbare rust-colored carpet and began a low-toned conversation about the latest developments in the art world. They sorted index card notes and consulted each other in muted undertones.

At the small desk near the door, I crossed my legs, clad in nonconformist blue jeans, and scanned a reply to a query about a teaching job in Kansas. It was a possibility to explore further, but there was nothing else particularly interesting in my day's mail. One letter was the weekly update from my mother. Two more brought replies from queries about teaching positions elsewhere in the country. Neither was exciting, but I still had faith that something interesting would come my way.

Across the room from the depths of the lop-sided armchair, Liz looked up from her pile of mail. She tossed one of her letters over to me. "This one looks more like your kind of thing," she offered generously. "You know I wrote to all the settlement schools in the southern mountains looking for a job with the children there. I wanted to use my child study major to work with Appalachian children the way my sister did at Pine Mountain in Kentucky. This answer is from the John C. Campbell School in Brasstown, North Carolina. It is not a school for children but an experiment in adult education in Appalachia, much more like what interests you. It would be a real opportunity to see a different part of the country and perhaps do something exciting there."

At that point another head poked through the hall door, laundry carton and box of cookies from home clutched with the mail. Stephie looked at Liz, catching the gist of the remark she had overheard. "I thought you were going to volunteer a year at one of those mountain schools yourself. Did you change your mind?"

"No," Liz replied thoughtfully. "Everyone in my family volunteered a year of service after college, and I wanted to do so as well, so I wrote to all the settlement schools, but so far I've had no luck in finding a place. I may have to go to Simmons and get my master's in social work before I find work that is right for me. However, Ellie wants to teach young adults, and this sounds interesting. It's modeled on the Scandinavian folk schools."

She turned to me and raised her eyebrows. "What do you think?" I was looking at the brochures the school had sent. A picture of a man who was walking behind a horse pulling a small plow was titled "I Sing Behind the Plow." The letter described a job in the craft department of the school, where they sold carvings by mail to support the teaching program. They offered a course in life skills to young adults of the mountains in a farm setting. The staff position paid $50 a month with room and board. It was a grand sum, which managed carefully would retire my college loan.

"It looks interesting to me," I answered. "I'll write and see what they say." Something about the prospect of such a different environment beckoned. It was a bit like going back in history to pioneer days. Farming and a bit of adventure appealed to me. I'd think about it. I liked the idea of a school that offered education in new life-styles, in a rural community. The prospect of new experiences was exciting for each of us, but we were all aware that we were in the process of separating from the closest friends we would ever have in life. We needed to hold on to relationships as we each chose a different path.

Throughout our years together, Ann, who had grown up in Savannah, had entertained us with tales of the Old South. She invited us to visit her family, see the gardens in bloom, and share her pleasure in her native countryside. Peg wanted to observe the building of the dams on southern rivers and the architecture of Old Southern mansions. Liz and I were interested in Franklin Roosevelt's great experiment in the Tennessee River valley and the ways in which it would affect life in the South. So a little later that month, the four of us decided to take a vacation together during our spring break and satisfy our curiosity about the South. Liz's father was a Unitarian minister on the governing board of a number of schools and colleges in the South. He contacted friends and schools along the Atlantic coast and in Tennessee to arrange overnights for us and offered the use of their family car for our trip. Liz's mother stocked the trunk of the blue Dodge sedan with cans of tuna, lunch meat, pork and beans, soup, crackers and cookies, and other picnic supplies to facilitate our jaunt. We were off for a two-week adventure.

The first day we drove from Poughkeepsie to Catonsville, Maryland. Several years earlier in preparation for college, Ann and I had spent three years at Saint Timothy's School, an Episcopal boarding school outside of Baltimore. It was a model of Victorian propriety where we received excellent intellectual, ethical, and religious training and indoctrination in self-discipline. In college, where we had all the freedom we needed, we regaled our friends with horror stories of the old-fashioned rules and regulations at boarding school. Liz and Peg had lived at home in Cambridge, Massachusetts, during their preparatory years and couldn't even imagine our experience. Nothing would do until we could show them the quaint and wonderful halls of Saint Tim's. We wrote ahead to see if we could spend the night in our old dormitory and received an invitation for an evening snack as well.

It was late as we drove up the tree-lined lane to the school. Memories of three happy adolescent years and many friends whispered from the overhanging boughs. I led the way up the porch steps of the silent Victorian "Big House." Ann had arrived earlier and saw the lights of the car coming up the lane. She had one hand on the doorknob ready to welcome us, relief from her lonely vigil. She took us back to the kitchen, where Miss Briscoe, the tiny graying housekeeper, met us with hugs, sandwiches, milk, and cookies, welcoming Liz and Peg as two of her girls. The hospitality fascinated them.Afterward we toured the dark halls covered with framed reproductions of European medieval religious art. We looked into the formal front parlor, which was always reserved for students to receive guests of the opposite sex on Sunday afternoons, and into the living room where we sang hymns on Sunday morning until it was time to go to church next door. Ann and I had trouble restraining our giggles as we showed our New England friends the cherished rooms and recalled our ridiculous encounters with dignified authority. We reminded them that the school motto, *Verité sans peur* (truth without fear), had enforced the honor code. Self-reporting of rule infractions at roll call encouraged responsibility and discipline. At last we went thankfully to our old beds in the front rooms of the Big House to prepare for a second day of travel toward the South.

The next morning we drove south around the landmarks in Washington D.C. and arrived at Williamsburg, Virginia, about noon. John D. Rockefeller had recently begun the elaborate restoration of the colonial village there. The rosy ambience of the completed buildings thoroughly impressed me, but I left my three friends to admire them and wandered away down a side road outside the walls around the Governor's Palace. There I took snapshots of unpainted shacks on land not yet reclaimed from poverty, an illustration of the gap between rich and poor.

That evening we arrived at Hampton Institute near Norfolk in time for one of the most beautiful sunsets I have ever witnessed. The sky, a deep crimson, was reflected in the sea, and the ships in contrast were silhouetted in black. Many distinguished alumni had graduated from this pioneer black college, founded in 1868. We arrived in time for the evening meal in a huge dining hall. The experience of being a minority in a sea of black faces was new to us. Although Ann insisted that she had never known any black college students, her charming ability to converse with anyone on any subject quickly dissolved barriers of race. We spent the night there in the home of one of the directors, who had been a classmate of Liz's dad at Harvard.

The next day we moved down Route 17 through North Carolina to Orton Plantation just outside Wilmington. We spent that night in the antebellum mansion that had belonged to Ann's aunt and uncle, and which her cousin now managed. Huge four-poster beds furnished our bedroom, which looked out across former rice fields, no longer flooded because competition from other countries made production unprofitable. In the morning we wandered under the huge live oak trees, festooned in Spanish moss, and breakfasted on grits, fried ham, and beaten biscuits. Ann's pleasure at showing us the beauty and joys of the South was contagious.

We drove down Route 1 into South Carolina the following day. We circled west to the Santee-Cooper River Basin, where a huge red-clay earthen dam was being built to provide flood control and an electric power plant. When completed it would provide inexpensive electricity for new industries in the area. The men were working twenty-four hour shifts in order to complete it as quickly as possible.

We were content to gaze down at the work below from the observation stand until Ann and Peg engaged in conversation with one of the foremen, who invited us down to the muddy bottom of the site. There we stood shoe-deep in sticky red clay as he explained the plan and the procedure for executing it. He was impressed that college girls were interested in his work and took the time to go into great detail, answering all our questions about the seventy-foot lock and allowing us to examine the tremendous dam and powerhouse close up.

We spent the rest of the day exploring Charleston and the coast of South Carolina. In the evening, we celebrated with a feast of southern cooking at an inn in Beaufort. As the sun set in the west, we took Ann to her parents' home in Savannah and settled ourselves in a small hotel nearby.

We breakfasted with Ann and headed for Tybee Island. On the beach we threw off our shoes and socks and danced joyfully, kicking up our heels in freedom. That day we looked over the many city squares that provide leisurely interruptions in travel around town, and we saw gracious old homes everywhere. Azalea bushes were in full bloom in multiple shades from pale pink to deep cerise. Gardens were bright with spring flowers, everything from tulips to narcissus to crocuses, violets, and pansies. Ann's parents entertained us at their home and Ann reminisced about her childhood there. Then because Mr. Nash had been in the business of supplying naval stores, we made a special trip to the waterfront docks and watched the loading of pine products on freighters to ship overseas that day. Reluctantly, on Wednesday we left Ann with her parents and continued the trip without her.

We drove back up the South Carolina coast to visit Penn School on Saint Helena Island. Liz's dad was on the board of directors there. Two elderly, maiden ladies from New England, the only white people on the island, welcomed us cordially. They were educating the black island children in a day school of which they were very proud. Delighted to have company, they spent the day showing us the beautiful island, their classrooms, and introducing their students.

As the sun rose early the next morning, we headed west on Route 28, following the border between two states, through Augusta, Georgia, and Anderson, South Carolina. We passed eroded cotton country where overused, underfertilized fields caused huge fissures. Sharecropper shacks stood in isolation amid gaunt, bare stalks of cotton, too poor to even warrant picking, and cornstalks, topped for cattle fodder. We waved to small black children playing in the naked broom-swept yards. On the small porches, older folk huddled out of the rain to escape the claustrophobia of crowded rooms inside and to watch cars pass on the road.

As we neared North Carolina, the mountains rose around us. In those years, the mountains of northern Georgia and Western

North Carolina were isolated and unique. Houses were distantly spaced. The road wound through small towns where graceful old two-story houses with ample porches and faded paint were reminiscent of better times. Along the narrow highway, new compact white houses were strung out farther and farther apart as we moved into the small-farming country of the uplands.

Franklin Roosevelt's plan to develop the Tennessee River valley promised to combat soil erosion, flooding, and poverty in the South. We wanted to see this experiment in progress. Promise of change filled the air as the wild dogwood brightened the hillsides. Fog filled the hollows, and mist covered the rolling tops of the hills. We had promised Ann we would find her family's rustic summer cottage in Highlands, and we ate a picnic lunch there in the company of squirrels carved in the porch railing. Then we continued west on U.S. Highway 64. As we climbed down from Highlands, we passed under the Bridal Veil Falls cascading over the twisting asphalt road that hugged the steep mountain. We drove along the highway toward Murphy, passing through Hayesville almost without noticing the town. We had no idea how close we were to the J. C. Campbell Folk School, where I had inquired about a job, but as rain blurred the windshield in a straight stretch of road that later I would know as Brasstown, Liz waved her hand off to the south guessing that the school was near. "Do you want to stop and find the Folk School?" she asked casually.

We were hoping to get as far as Chattanooga before dark, and evening was coming fast, so I replied, "No, I'll probably never hear any more about that job anyway."

Beyond Brasstown, the road followed the Hiwassee River. At one point, it curved sharply over Scott Laney Mountain, where we looked down into the valley on our left. Peg, who was driving, pulled off the road as soon as she was able and turned to Liz with tears in her eyes. "Won't you please drive for a while? It really made me woozy and sick when we looked down back there."

They changed places, and we drove into Murphy to look for shelter for the night. The square in the center of town had a water fountain, troughs and hitching posts for the horses, and a war memorial to the veterans of World War I. On the south side of the square was the four-story yellow brick Hotel Regal. The commercial hotel did not look too friendly, and Murphy did not seem to offer much in the way of interest for three college-educated Yankee girls on that rainy afternoon in 1941. In addition, we had promised our mothers we would stay with friends along the way or in YWCAs, so we decided to press on to Chattanooga.

We drove about twenty miles farther in North Carolina through rolling farmland and wooded hillsides. As we passed into Tennessee, a sign greeted us reading: "Welcome to the State of Tennessee. No Speed Limit. Drive Carefully at Your Own Speed." For me it seemed to express the spirit of the frontier West, without limits.

Almost immediately, the change in scenery shocked us. We were in a barren wasteland of denuded red-clay hills. Not a bit of vegetation was in sight. It was so devastated, eroded, and strange as to be almost unbelievable. There were no houses, no people in sight, just miles and miles of red-clay desert without even an oasis. We stopped as soon as we saw a small store at the side of the road.

We went in. "What happened here?" we demanded breathlessly, expecting to hear of a great disaster.

"You must be new to these parts," the storekeeper said with a smile. "Everyone stops here to ask me about it when they see this for the first time. Back in the early part of the 1900s, the Tennessee Copper Company began to mine the ore here. They cut the timber to fire the smelters. Sulfuric acid fumes from the furnaces killed all the vegetation and nothing grows back." We thanked the storekeeper, bought some crackers and drinks for the rest of the trip, and went on our way, shaking our heads in disgust.

In Cleveland, Tennessee, down a twisting road beside the Ocoee River from the Copper Basin, we stopped for supper at a small restaurant in town. Crisp fried chicken, creamed corn, green beans cooked with salt pork, fluffy mashed potatoes, hot biscuits, and apple cobbler cost us each twenty-five cents. It was our introduction to "country cooking." After the shock of devastated land, it somewhat restored our sense of the goodness of life and gave us strength for the balance of the trip to Chattanooga.

Before continuing our trip the next morning, we drove a short distance over into Alabama to add one more state to our list of those visited. Then we drove north through Tennessee and observed the building of Watts Bar Dam on the Tennessee River. We toured the area that would become the town of Oak Ridge, not yet off limits to the public. The atomic bomb would later be developed there.

Outside of Knoxville, we visited overnight with the family of an engineer at Norris Dam. He was a friend of Liz's dad. After supper he asked, "Would you girls like to see slides of the work in the Tennessee Valley?" We replied with enthusiasm, and he treated us to a preview of the growth and development that was expected. Flood-controlling dams and hydroelectric power plants were being built on all the tributaries of the Tennessee River. "Locks at the dams will make it possible for riverboats to come all the way upriver from the Gulf of Mexico to Knoxville," he told us.

The next day this scholarly friend took us on a tour of Norris Dam. It was a beautiful, tall structure of light-colored cement. The grain of the wooden forms into which the cement had been poured still showed plainly on the walls of the dam. The use of the wooden forms was new to me, and I was impressed by the juxtaposition of the natural and the man-made in this engineering project.

Leaving Tennessee, we drove through a corner of Kentucky, so we could say we had been there also. We stopped to picnic by a country stream that ran black with coal dust from mines in Harlan County. It reminded us again of the devastating effects of mining on the environment. Looking up as we drove on through a narrow valley between precipitous mountains, we were in awe of long white banners reading "Jesus saves" stretched from one side of the valley to the other. Peg commented, "The South is certainly a land of contrasts. Hope in the here and now and faith in the hereafter."

Back in Poughkeepsie for our final semester at college, I realized we had accomplished many of our goals for the trip. Almost effortlessly, the trip validated the life choices I would make. We would all have wonderful memories of this special time together. The South and the opportunities there had won my heart. I had fallen in love with the mountains, the hospitality of Southerners, and the prospect of change. When a letter came from Louise Pitman at the Folk School offering me a job, I quickly made a few inquiries about the school and then wrote to say that I would arrive in September, on Labor Day weekend.

Doris Ulmann. Photo courtesy of the John C. Campbell Folk School Archives, Brasstown, North Carolina.

"Mrs. Campbell's blue eyes peered kindly and quizzically at me through rimless glasses, one eye squinting slightly."

THE JOHN C. CAMPBELL FOLK SCHOOL was sixteen years old and I was twenty-two the year I traveled many hundreds of miles to explore a world very different from the familiar culture in which I had grown up.

After a carefree summer with family and friends on the rocky coast of Maine, I rode trains and a bus to Vermont, where I met my college roommate Liz and her brother Caleb. He had graduated from Harvard the previous year and spent time in California. He had returned home to convert an ancient wood-bodied station wagon into a makeshift van in which he could live. He and Liz were taking it to California, and they offered me a ride as far as Cleveland, Ohio.

Liz and Caleb were my good friends, and during our college years, I spent part of each summer vacation visiting their family in Maine. Liz and I had roomed together with Ann and Peg in different combinations for four years. Caleb had been my date for Junior Prom and had tried to teach me sailing skills off the rocky shore of his parents' summer home in Southwest Harbor. Their offer of a ride was too good to refuse. As we drove from Vermont across New York State into Ohio, we engaged in a variety of serious discussions about life amid some light-hearted laughter.

After an impromptu swim in Lake Erie, Caleb and Liz dropped me at the train station in Cleveland. I planned to finish my journey alone in a continued patchwork pattern of archaic rail connections. A train took me to Cincinnati, where I spent a weary night in the teeming terminal, waiting for the connecting train to Lexington, Kentucky. As I battled exhaustion and the loneliness of parting with good friends, I consoled myself with a sense of adventure and curiosity about my future in a new job with unknown people in the southern mountains.

We rolled east to Lexington and south across the bluegrass country of Kentucky. I dozed against the cold train window and wondered fitfully where this adventure was leading me. Intermittently I woke to look out at the country as we moved into the Appalachian foothills on the edge of a coal-mining region and then into eastern Tennessee and south to the state's corner, bordering Georgia.

Approaching Chattanooga, the tracks curved around the river at Moccasin Bend, hugging the side of Lookout Mountain on the east and moving upstream beside the Tennessee River on the west. A smoky haze hung over the city, residue of the iron and steel industries, which were busy supplying the war that was consuming Europe.

The station platform was dark, dusky, and empty as I, the solitary remaining passenger on the coach, climbed down. Far up the tracks, the big steam locomotive puffed slowly as if it were as glad as I was to complete the trip. Not seeing a redcap porter, I picked up my suitcase, assorted books, and overnight case and entered the station lobby. It seemed quaint in its simplicity. No one else was waiting there, and the ticket windows were closed. The separate rest rooms and water fountains for *white* and *colored* had profoundly shocked me on our trip last spring; the discrimination was still offensive to me, but I was no longer surprised. I walked through the station and found myself on a wide brick-paved street.

It was quiet that Sunday evening as I looked around to orient myself. Signal Mountain rose behind me and, ahead, Lookout Mountain stood guard over the city. Directly across from the depot stood a red brick garage with a broad sign overhead reading "TRAILWAYS." The bus station was exactly where Louise Pitman had told me it would be when she wrote me to say that I had the job. She told me that she would meet the bus when it made its run from Chattanooga to Murphy, and I found that all was as she had described it. I marched confidently toward the bus, which stood with its engine panting. The driver motioned me to the small ticket booth, indicating with a friendly wave that he would wait. I bought my ticket to Murphy and climbed on.

There were only a few passengers, scattered on both sides of the aisle. The driver punched my ticket and stowed my suitcase in an open space behind his seat. A lean young fellow in overalls sat directly behind the driver. I chose the third seat on the right side of the bus where there was room for my smaller things on the worn, brown plastic seat beside me. I leaned my tired head against yet another window to rest.

Streetlights in the deepening dusk evoked a lonely aura in the quiet Sunday evening streets of Chattanooga. We stopped at the outskirts of the city and picked up a young woman carrying a baby and holding a toddler by the hand. She sat down in the front seat across from the driver and waved to an older woman standing on the curb. Awkwardly, she held up the little boy's hand, so he could also wave to the woman, probably his grandmother. As we pulled away the young woman wiped tears from her eyes with the back of her hand and waved until we were far out of sight. I felt a twinge of longing for my own mother, whom I had left so far behind three days ago.

There were no more stops until, after almost an hour, we pulled into the bus station on the small town square in Cleveland, Tennessee. There the bus driver left his seat and came back to the young woman. "I'll hep you down with your young'uns," he offered. She accepted his help and climbed down carefully. A boy, who looked no older than twenty, met her. They embraced shyly, but the little boy squealed with delight as his father lifted him high in the air. The remaining passengers exchanged smiles. Their friendly informality was like that of the country people I had left in New England, but it was certainly different from the brusque manners of New Yorkers. There we respected the privacy of people we did not know and ignored feelings and individual relationships. I liked this atmosphere. No one seemed to be in a hurry.

A lean, old man in a starched white shirt, string tie, and iron-creased overalls climbed aboard, holding his broad-brimmed black hat in front of him with both hands. He sidled past me and took a seat toward the back of the bus. His old-fashioned manner, dress, and quiet dignity reminded me of the gentle grace of a character from Shakespeare's England.

The driver revved the engine, and we rumbled off into the black night. Leaving the lights of Cleveland behind, we made a few more stops in the dark to let people on or off as they traveled just a few miles from store or church or friend toward home. A moon rose above the trees on the steep ridge to the left of the road, and soon I could see the pale, muddy ripples and swirls of Lake Ocoee on the right. Then the road narrowed and began to twist and climb into the Ocoee Gorge.

At times, I could see the river in the moonlight to the right of the winding two-lane macadam road that clung to the steep hewn-rock cliff on our left. As we moved upstream, the water appeared shallow and the river became wider, strewn with boulders. Eventually we emerged from the river gorge and climbed to the plateau of the Copper Basin desert.

The naked landscape stretched out in the moonlight on both sides of the road. The memory of the rainy afternoon during last spring vacation as we traveled here came back to me vividly. The thought of the wanton waste disgusted me again. I hated the irresponsibility of the mining companies that had stripped the land by clear-cutting all the trees. Without vegetation, the bare red-clay soil eroded into great gullies and washed downstream to fill the riverbed and cause floods. I missed the company of my friends who felt as I did about this outrage. However, on this nighttime journey I dozed again, exhausted, conserving my energy for Brasstown.

More than four hours from Chattanooga, we swung into the town square in Murphy. At the intersection of the two main streets was a large fountain set in a small park and surrounded by metal hitching posts. I stood up to see it, glad to stretch my legs. It was a memorial to the dead of World War I. I prayed quickly that we would not really become involved in the present war in Europe.

On the southwest corner of the square stood the yellow-brick Regal Hotel, four stories tall. For years it had provided lodging and meals for commercial travelers of all sorts. Last spring Liz and Peg and I had passed up the opportunity to stop there. The ground floor of the old hotel now included several small shops facing the square. The bus station occupied a corner of one of these. Although it was just after eleven o'clock at night, two ladies were standing on the sidewalk as we rolled to a stop. The shorter lady, who stood confidently erect, offered her hand in greeting. "I'm Olive Campbell," she said in a broad Boston accent. "You must be Eleanor Lambert."

Then she turned to her companion and introduced Louise Pitman, a tall, strong middle-aged woman with a firm handshake and a direct manner. Louise asked, "Have you had any supper, Eleanor?"

"No, there wasn't any time between the train and the bus, and there was no dining car on the train," I replied.

Mrs. Campbell said cheerfully, "Well then, we must go in."

Louise took me by the arm, and I went with them into the brightly lit ice cream parlor. Several small round tables, surrounded by the wire-backed chairs so characteristic of ice cream parlors everywhere, stood in the middle of the room. A closed ticket booth for the bus station filled a small corner. Across the back of the room was a glass-fronted bakery counter.

Mrs. Campbell introduced the pretty, auburn-haired young woman behind the counter. "This is Margaret Holland, who takes care of the shop and bus station. Our Mountain Valley Cooperative has opened this store in Murphy to sell ice cream and other dairy products. They stay open until the bus from Chattanooga comes in although they usually close at eleven. I'm afraid there is really nothing left to eat, but Margaret said she would make you a large milk shake. Will that do?" I accepted gratefully.

In the light of the shop, Mrs. Campbell appeared elderly and frail, but her lively manner and quick speech conveyed the impression of energy and intense interest in her surroundings. An engraved silver headband secured her short white hair, combed plainly to one side. The years of travel through the southern mountains on horseback with her husband that had sparked her interest in the education of isolated mountain people had merely softened her New England accent a little.

We sat at one of the small white metal tables. The rounded wire-backed chair kept my sagging body at attention. I revived a bit as Margaret brought my chocolate milk shake topped with whipped cream and a cherry. Mrs. Campbell's blue eyes peered kindly and quizzically at me through rimless glasses, one eye squinting slightly. "Do we call you Eleanor, or do you have a nickname?" she asked.

"Ellie, please call me Ellie—everyone does," I replied nervously, eager to appear friendly and informal.

I looked around the store trying to notice details. There were no other customers this late at night. Behind the counter, Margaret was obviously getting ready to close up and go home. She washed all the dishes and cleaned off the counters. Then she removed a sweater from the coat rack in the corner and put it around her shoulders. She stood behind the counter without comment, but I felt intrusive and reluctant to impose too long.

Mrs. Campbell, however, was talkative. "Mountain Valley Cooperative is a Folk School project that encourages small farmers to make a better living by selling milk and eggs locally. We collect the farm products within a fifty-mile radius, processing and marketing them, and returning the profits to the members. The ice cream parlor is an attempt to reach town people and take money back to the farms," she explained.

Louise Pitman's broad forehead was framed with brown hair combed back and fastened in a bun at the back of her neck. She watched me kindly and sensed my discomfort. She smiled and reassured me heartily, "There's no need to hurry. Just enjoy your shake. It's a small enough supper, and you must be tired." Her friendliness and intuition boded well for a future relationship, I thought. I felt comfortable with both her and Mrs. Campbell as they welcomed me after my long journey. I was glad to get the background information Mrs. Campbell offered with such pride.

Soon we piled into the Folk School's big blue Chevrolet sedan. Louise drove and Mrs. Campbell sat beside her, half-turned in the seat to include me in the conversation. My bags and I spread out on the back seat. "How far do we go?" I asked as I peered through the night, trying to see the countryside to which I had committed a year of my life.

"The Folk School is in Brasstown, eight miles up the Hiwassee River from Murphy," Louise explained as she maneuvered the curves on narrow, black macadam U.S. Highway 64. "We are pretty much a community unto ourselves. Our social life is mostly at the school and with the people who live in Brasstown."

"We shop only occasionally in Murphy," Mrs. Campbell added. "We raise almost all our own food on the farm."

Answering and asking questions as we rode, I began feeling my way into these new relationships.

Finally, Louise said, "We're almost there." We made a sharp right turn beside a small country store, onto a gravel road, and over a wooden bridge. In the pale moonlight I could see tall corn growing right up to the road edge on both sides of the car, seeming to close us off from the rest of the world.

"This is the Folk School property," Mrs. Campbell announced.

"How large is the school?" I asked.

"We have about 360 acres, some in woodland, some pasture, and the rest in crops. This year we will probably make a record number of bushels of corn to the acre. The school is a demonstration farm for the county. We have several houses, barns, and a shop, but the main building is Keith House, where you'll be staying. It is the girls' dormitory also. Louise and I live in Farm House."

About one hundred yards beyond a sharp U-curve in the road, we turned into the driveway of Keith House. Louise parked and got out of the car quickly. Mrs. Campbell turned and bade me a cheery good-night, settling herself to stay in the car. Louise took my bags from the back seat and led me toward the entrance to the house. Through the darkness of a country night unlit by streetlights, I sensed a three-story building of light-colored clap-board. There were almost no lights visible in the house. It was dark and quiet. We went in through a dimly lit, square entry hall paneled in wide pine boards. Then we climbed up a long flight of broad hardwood stairs to a silent second floor.

At the top of the stairs, we passed a simple bathroom, and next to it Louise pushed open the wooden door of a small bed-room. These were my accommodations. The room was plainly furnished with a low narrow bed covered with a patchwork quilt, a chest of drawers, a small washstand, and straight chair. A wooden lamp with a dim light bulb was on the bedside table. Louise explained quietly that the school limited the lighting to 25-watt light bulbs out of respect for the students who had grown up in homes without electricity.

"They are accustomed to oil lamps and will probably return

to that type of lighting, so we don't want them to get used to electricity," she said.

A heavy hemp rope attached to a sturdy iron ring in the wall lay coiled beneath two wide, small-paned windows. "If there is a fire in the night, you simply throw that out the window and slide down it to the ground," Louise explained. "In the morning at six o'clock, a cowbell will ring in the hallway outside your door. Get dressed and go down two flights of stairs to the dining room. Introduce yourself to Miss Gaines, the housemother, and to the students and enjoy your breakfast. I will see you soon after."

With that, Louise left me. Surrounded by silence, I felt abandoned, but relieved not to have to converse further. I needed time to stop traveling and assimilate my impressions and the information I had gleaned about my new world. I had arrived in Brasstown. I crept gratefully into bed, stretching full-length to savor the cool pleasure of clean sheets after two nights of travel. For a moment, I experienced a strange sense that I could not be the same person who had come all the way from Maine in three days. Would I ever again know my way around the streets of New York City, which had been familiar to me all my life? Would the academia in which I had immersed myself fade into a blurred past? Now I was face-to-face with an unknown future, promised to it for a year. I was too tired to sleep at once, and I lay wide-eyed, wondering if I had chosen foolishly and what the future would hold. Lazily I reviewed the kaleidoscope of images that had brought me here and that now continued to float through my mind. I laid aside the vision of sliding down the thick hemp rope and tried to imagine the sound of the cowbell destined to wake me too soon. Then I fell into the deep sleep of exhaustion.

❦ *Morning Song* ❦

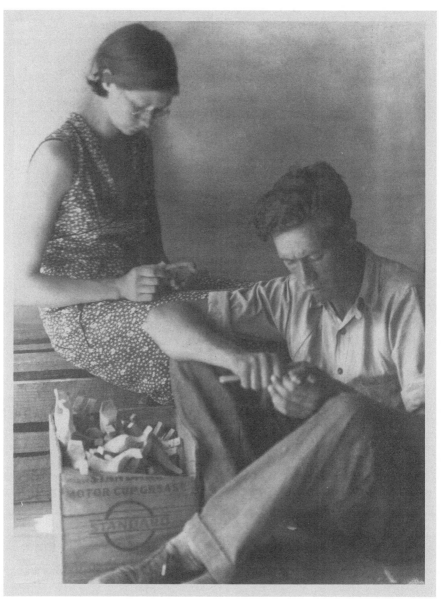

"Blocks for the wood carvings were given out to carvers in the community who carved them and brought them back for approval."

THE INSISTENT SOUND of the cowbell woke me to a gray dawn. For a moment, I didn't remember where I was. Then the reality of my surroundings came to me in a rush of adrenaline. With awareness came curiosity. I scrambled out of bed.

Quickly I chose a skirt of white calico print with a pattern of tiny scarlet flowers and green leaves. It slipped easily over my head and gathered at my waist in the broomstick style of the day. Adding a white blouse that wasn't too wrinkled, I finished dressing. I grinned at myself in the tiny mirror over the washstand, brushed my mousy brown hair, and scrubbed my face to put some color in my cheeks; I felt almost ready for whatever the day would bring.

There were footsteps and muffled voices passing in the hallway outside my door. Bashfully I waited for them to go by before I went out, silently closing the bedroom door behind me. As I started down the stairway, the steps creaked ominously, but no one materialized ahead of me as I tiptoed along, trying to make myself invisible in the semidarkness. My anxiety heightened as the breakfast gong in the dining room chimed once more. My breath caught fearfully. I was going to be late. There was a second flight of stairs below me.

I was relieved as I reached the last steps between the two dark walls. A large basement room opened brightly in front of me at the bottom of the stairs. The concrete floor was painted dark red, and high windows on two sides of the room looked out above ground. I paused and looked around, noticing each cheerful detail of the room. Plants hung from wrought iron brackets at the small-paned windows. A trailing red geranium graced one opening; a lush green plant with purple flowers filled the other. Rough orange pottery filled the shelves of a sideboard cabinet, where the lower doors were stenciled with a colorful geometric design in European fashion.

There were four cross-legged pine tables. Short benches marked the ends of each, and longer benches lined the sides. Three tables were empty, but across the room the breakfast group sat at the fourth table. The smell of fresh coffee and a fruity tang of juice wafted a greeting.

The housemother, Miss Ruth B. Gaines, sat on the short bench with her back to me. Her round, aging body overflowed the bench. Without looking around, she bid me gruffly, "Come in and have a seat. We're ready to begin."

Then she half-turned and motioned me to sit down on the long bench at her left side. Her brown eyes crinkled at the corners, and an amused smile sneaked across her mouth. Seven girls seated around the table looked me over with curiosity. The girl next to me moved over to make room. She was thin and a bit older than the others. Her brown hair was pulled back severely and tied at the back of her head. Her snapping dark eyes met mine, and her tanned face lighted with a friendly smile. She offered her hand openly and briskly in welcome.

"I'm Leila Stalcup. I come from Martin's Creek, just up the Little Brasstown Road. I've finished school, but I'm working here, helping Miss Gaines. Maybe she'll make me into a dietitian like herself." She glanced at Miss Gaines, teasing, but didn't get a response, just a faint, motherly smile.

I was grateful for Leila's forthright introduction, which encouraged me to respond in turn. Then I scanned the table as Miss Gaines asked each girl to introduce herself. Across from me sat a small fair-skinned girl, who grinned shyly. Her bright blond hair was cut short in a Dutch boy bob. When the attention shifted to her, she reddened with embarrassment that she was in the spotlight and gruffly murmured, "Annie Laurie, I'm from Mills River." In more relaxed fashion, Helen, Vess, Sophie, Maggie, and a tiny impish girl, who called herself "Peavine" followed suit. Each one introduced herself by quietly attaching the name of the community or county from which she came. It gave reassurance of identity and a sense of belonging.

The table was set with heavy tan china, bordered with a thin brown line. A small glass of tomato juice punctuated each place, and a large tureen of oatmeal steamed in front of Miss Gaines. She returned thanks in a brief blessing to the Lord, and then deftly scooped the porridge into bowls. We passed them around the table and poured on honey and thick cream.

I seized an opportunity to ask about the plant with the purple flowers. "It's a mother's tear," they chorused, eager to help me out. "It puts out little brown cones that we can plant again when it finishes blooming."

There was silence and a clinking of spoons as everyone began to eat. When given an opportunity, Peavine ventured the question, timidly, as if rehearsed, "Do you know Brooklyn? They say you come from New York, and Brooklyn is there."

"I know where it is, but I lived outside New York City on Long Island, not near Brooklyn, which is across the East River from New York."

"Oh dear, I have a brother at the Navy Yard in Brooklyn. I was hoping you might know him," she lamented.

"Sorry," I replied, and no one even smiled.

It was good to be accepted so casually. I might have been a neighbor dropping in on a daily basis instead of a strange college graduate from New York, a place known only in name. I sensed that they accepted me based on what I could do or say rather than on my birthplace or college.

The homemade tomato juice was symbolic of the strangeness I felt at breakfast. I had always enjoyed fresh orange juice, even in college, but, of course, orange juice was a "fureigner," like me. Tomato juice came from the plentiful bounty of summer gardens. Grateful for its cool red tartness, I drained my glass.

Small talk about the day to come slipped easily between polite questions about my journey. The geography of my trip from the northeast down through Ohio, Kentucky, and Tennessee meant little to anyone except Miss Gaines, whose original home was near Springfield, Massachusetts. Their world was too small for the girls to imagine places outside of the mountains.

All the girls except Leila were new at the Folk School, ready to start a year different from any they had experienced in the rural mountain schools from which they had come. Most had graduated from high school with adequate knowledge of basic subjects. Here they would "learn by doing" all the skills relative to country life.

"What does each of you want to learn here?" I asked.

"Nutrition . . . art . . . cooking . . . homemaking," came back the chorus.

Mischievous Annie Laurie said soberly, "Square dancing," and grinned at the others.

Someone chimed in, "Singing. I liked debate in high school, too."

An air of quiet dignity and shy kindness surrounded the table as we accomplished the task of polishing off a hearty breakfast. Then we heard an outside door close noisily. Without comment, Miss Gaines disappeared into the kitchen.

"The dairy boys have finished milking and are here with our milk," Leila explained. "We have to give them breakfast in the kitchen. They've been up since five, and they're starved, but they smell like the cows." She wrinkled her nose and shook her head gently.

With the departure of Miss Gaines, some of the warmth left the room. We finished eating, cleared the table, and the dish-washing team took over. "Time to go upstairs for Morning Song," Leila told me.

Then, responding to my puzzled expression, she explained, "It's the first class of the day. We'll all be there and so will the staff. We sing some old songs and learn something new, sometimes about some other country or perhaps some nature study. I'll be up as soon as I finish helping in the kitchen." Then politely she added, "It's nice to meet you."

The other girls disappeared up the two flights of stairs to make their beds and prepare for the school day. I went up alone, slowly, to the main floor. I could hear cheery voices in the living room exchanging greetings as the staff converged from various houses on the grounds or from the community.

Feeling inherently shy, I stood in the doorway and surveyed the scene. The room was paneled in a board-and-batten style with white pine, which had darkened some with fourteen years of use. There was a large rock fireplace with a heavy roughhewn wood mantel held in place by jutting rocks. In the corner beyond the fireplace was a small spinet piano. On the bench in front of it sat a neat woman in khaki skirt and navy coat-sweater. Her dark hair, touched with gray, was drawn back in a schoolmarm bun at the nape of her neck, and she was shuffling through a pile of sheet music on the stand in front of her. Set back in a semicircle facing the piano were several rows of straight-back wooden chairs with woven seats of split oak similar to the chairs made by the country people I had known in New England.

In the far corner of the room under a window, built-in storage benches made a cozy L. A table, holding a newspaper and a large pottery jug of goldenrod, sat in the space provided in front of the benches, and a lamp hung overhead. Floor-to-ceiling bookcases hugged two walls; packed with books in a variety of shapes, sizes, and colorful covers, they invited exploration.

Four wide double-hung windows looked out on the front entrance and parking lot. They were multipaned, hung with straight curtains that were handwoven of soft red with a small geometric-patterned white border. The spaces between the windows held oil paintings, one a mountain landscape and the other a log building in a woodland setting. There were two photographs: a boy walking behind a plow and a picture of Grundtvig, the founder of Danish folk schools. Elsewhere there were a few rocking chairs and a long library table with a bench behind it. It was a pleasant, inviting room in which small groups of people were congregating.

Much to my relief, as I waited in the doorway bashful and unnoticed, Louise Pitman appeared. She greeted me in the same hearty way that had reassured me the previous night. I noticed that even as she took charge, she had a gentle, reticent manner. "Well, you look rested. Did you have a good night and a good breakfast? Now that you've met Miss Gaines and the girls, I want to be sure you meet everyone else this morning." She took me by the arm and turned, just as a sun-tanned man dressed in blue jeans and open-necked shirt crossed the room with a bouncy step and an out-stretched hand.

"Georg, this is Ellie Lambert. She came in on the bus last night, and she'll be helping me in the craft department. Ellie, this is Georg Bidstrup, our farm manager."

"Vell, vell," He greeted me with a broad Danish accent. "It vill be good to have another Wassar girl here at the school," he said jovially, as a small lady, with graying hair swept back from her face and secured with a woven, red headband, stepped up beside him. She was dressed in a peasant blouse and full, red skirt with a small, embroidered white apron. "This is my wife, Margaret," he said, putting his arm around her shoulders protectively, and contracting her name of Marguerite. "She has been our only Wassar graduate up until now."

She extended her hand in greeting. "It is good to have a sister alumna here. You'll be a great help to Louise. I read that you managed the business part of the yearbook, the 'Vassarion,' this past spring. That was a useful experience, I'm sure." Marguerite smiled graciously.

I smiled also, but I cringed inwardly, not wanting to be labeled as strictly business-oriented. The design and content of the yearbook had been my primary interest, but the task of selling advertising spaces and sponsors had netted a profit, which we, as yearbook staff, had been able to divide. My practical needs had outweighed my creativity. I opened my mouth to explain my position, but Louise gave me a slight tug and moved me forward toward the next person. I returned the smile and simply thanked her.

"We'll start Morning Song in just a minute as soon as Mrs. Campbell gets here," Marguerite said, looking at her watch. Then she bustled off toward the office that opened from the opposite side of the room.

Everyone in the room turned as the outside door in the hallway clanged open and a voice sang facetiously, "Heigh ho, heigh ho, it's off to work we go." Mrs. Campbell hurried in with a small basket on her arm. It held carving tools, and a half-carved figure resembling Saint Francis peered over the edge.

"Good morning, good morning to each and everyone of you," she greeted, moving quickly as she motioned the roomful to their places. Students filed in singly or in groups. The "girls" came down from upstairs, the half dozen "boys" slipped in from the terrace outside where they had lounged, waiting for the session to begin. Everyone sat in the semicircular rows of chairs facing the piano. Immediately we launched into "We Gather Together to Ask the Lord's Blessing" with Marguerite and Mrs. Campbell leading the singing with enthusiasm.

Introductions followed. Louise introduced me first, and I stood shyly to acknowledge the welcome. Next, the pianist stood and introduced herself. "I'm Harriet Cornwell, originally from Iowa. Here I'm the secretary and play the piano for Morning Song and Friday Night Games. My husband, Gwen, and I live in the community. He works for the Co-op now, but we are building a house and will be farming." She sat down, ready to accompany the singing as needed.

A short, swarthy man with a shock of jet-black hair rose near the newspaper table in the corner and said, "I'm Harry Cary. My wife, June, and our boys live in Pine View Cottage. You and the girls will have to walk down and see us. June is the school artist and she loves to have company in the afternoons when the boys are napping." I acknowledged the invitation with a nod and made a mental note to look them up.

We sang again; this time it was a ballad, "Barbary Allen," which seemed familiar to everyone but me. Then Mrs. Campbell cleared her throat and stood to tell the class about Grundtvig, the founder of the folk school movement in Denmark in the mid-1800s. Her genteel Boston accent softened as she told her story.

"Grundtvig lived from 1783 to 1872. He spent his eighty-nine years as a priest, poet, historian, teacher, and reformer, and he influenced Danish life and thought more than did any other one man. Out of his love for Denmark, out of his love for her people, he conceived the theory of the Danish folk school. I think he would find it a very helpful model for schools in this country, especially for these schools whose goal is to prepare young people for a successful farming life." Her earnest sincerity and hope for better standards of living in the mountains were evident. Most of the students listened attentively as she sketched her dreams of the future.

As Mrs. Campbell came to the end of her homily, a latecomer appeared. He was dressed in khaki Jodhpur riding pants tucked into high-laced leather boots. Fair-skinned with thinning sandy-colored hair, he wore round wire-rimmed glasses and looked the part of a surveyor.

"This is Mr. Deschamps," she said, introducing him to the roomful. "Boys, he'll be teaching surveying and farm machinery maintenance. If we have anything that needs fixing, he will take care of it and teach you how to do the same on your own farms some day."

Mr. Deschamps acknowledged the introduction in a heavy Belgian accent. He accepted the day's list of small repairs from Georg and observed, "It seems we have a little leak to fix in the water system, two broken windowpanes at Mill House, and Miss Gaines wants us to cure the squeaky hinges on the laundry room door. We will learn by doing those chores, boys." He raised his hand in farewell.

Georg responded in promise, "The boys and I vill join you in a few minutes, Leon."

We sang another folk song, chosen by a student, and were dismissed without further ceremony to go to classes or to work. Louise and I departed for the woodworking shop. Walking out the front door of Keith House, we crossed the naturalized wooded space encircled by the driveway and took a short path to the gravel road that bisected the school property.

Directly across the road from Keith House was the rock building that housed the shop. Blocks for the woodcarvings were sawed there. The blocks were given out to carvers in the community who carved them and brought them back for approval. Then the carvings returned to the shop to be finished, packed, and shipped from the business office.

Morning Song had given me a strong impression of the Folk School as an interesting combination of cosmopolitan staff, country life, and mountain culture. Putting that idea aside, I went in with Louise to begin learning the intricacies of a craft enterprise that helped support the school.

🌿 *Shop Talk* 🌿

"We went into the next room. It was almost filled with looms."

THE SHOP BUILDING was a combination of rock and wood frame. It contained the heart of the Folk School craft enterprise. Louise and I went up a few steps and opened the front door into a large room that combined several different facets of the business. I could feel her modest pride as we walked across the room to her desk area on the far side.

Abruptly, she became completely businesslike. Opening the top drawer of the old-fashioned wooden file cabinet standing next to her desk, she explained, "These are the folders for each of the retail shops around the country that order and sell Folk School carvings. Behind them are the retail sales folders for customers who order directly from the Folk School catalog or from advertisements in such magazines as *Better Homes and Gardens*."

In other drawers were folders for the Southern Highland Handicraft Guild and for each of the institutions and groups around the country that sponsored benefit sales in support of the school. It was organized so that even through the lingering haze of exhaustion, I knew I could easily manage the system.

Louise looked at the pile of mail on her desk and excused herself. "Do you mind if I take care of these for a minute while you look around? Just prowl a bit and see what you can find to ask me about."

Near the entrance in a corner opposite Louise's desk was a long table well lighted on two sides by rows of large windows. Two tall cans, one of shellac and the other labeled "Sheen Coat," stood beside glass jars holding paintbrushes and emitting a pleasant acrid odor. A stack of fine sandpaper and a large roll of #0000 steel wool were grouped in the center of the spotted and stained wooden tabletop.

A pile of unfinished woodcarvings huddled in the center: pigs, geese, and napkin rings, ready for wood filler. I leaned over, placing both hands on the edge of the worn surface to get a closer view of the collection. The pigs were of all sizes, including hogs and fat sows along with a variety of piglets—sucking, running, sitting, or lying on their backs, chubby legs in the air. There were large geese with necks outstretched as if in search of food. The napkin rings were of darker wood and represented squirrels with their centers cut out to hold individual napkins.

Several straight-backed chairs stood around this table ready for workers, students who paid for tuition and board by doing various jobs at the school on a rotating basis. Although I felt shy and hesitant about meeting them as I invaded their territory, I was anxious for a little life in the room. I glanced at Louise's broad back as she sat, still engrossed in the work at her desk.

Across the back of the room stretched a broad, tall counter under a row of high windows. On it was a large roll of binder twine on a spindle. Away from the corner walls, at the free end of the counter and fastened securely was a large iron dispenser with a roll of brown wrapping paper. It turned to allow sheets of any size to be torn off. On a shelf underneath were cardboard cartons of all shapes and sizes and stacks of old newspapers. All the equipment for shipping orders was located on this counter.

The small windows looked out on a wooded bank that sloped up the hill behind the shop. My eyes rose above the trees, seeking a small patch of sky. There was no sign of life. The hill rose above my line of vision, closing me off with a sense of entrapment. This would be my exclusive territory. I would spend many hours here wrapping small carvings to ship. What in the world had I been thinking of when I agreed to come so far to do such routine work? I looked out with homesick misgivings at the environment in which I found myself. I thought of Liz and Caleb driving west. I missed friends and the stimulation of college life. Depressed, I inadvertently allowed a deep sigh to escape me.

Quickly Louise responded, asking kindly, "Are you tired, Ellie?" I smiled and shook my head, wordless past the lump in my throat. Turning, I explored the fourth wall where shallow cupboards held shelves of finished carvings arranged in families. There were rows of dogs—cocker spaniels, bulldogs, great danes, hounds, every conceivable kind of puppy. Horses pranced on another shelf. Idly, I whimsically rearranged a few with those of pure white wood in pursuit of the "bad guys" carved of dark, walnut wood.

Louise looked up as I finished my survey. In her most businesslike mode she explained, "It will be your task to select the carvings needed to fill an order from those shelves." Patiently and deliberately she rehearsed the entire procedure, from reading the order received in the mail to placing the package ready for the Brasstown post office by the outside door. Her devotion to details unmistakably conveyed the importance of following procedure carefully, and my stomach did a gentle flip-flop of anxiety.

A light knock on the glass pane in the shop door and then a turn of the doorknob mercifully interrupted us. A small girl with light brown hair and a sprinkling of freckles across her nose came in. With just a glance toward us and a murmured "Good morning," she went toward the finishing table, determined not to intrude. However, Louise intercepted her with an introduction. Jewell Sales turned to greet me with an extended hand.

"Pleased to meet you," she said. "The others will be here soon. I saw them over at Keith House as I walked up the road." Without further pleasantries, she sat down at the long table by the window and began to assemble the carvings she would be putting the "finish" on that day.

"While you get started, I'm going to introduce Ellie to Herman and show her the rest of the shop," Louise explained in the quiet, authoritative way to which I was quickly becoming accustomed.

We went through a doorway next to the packing desk into a dark windowless room stacked with lumber and redolent with its rich dusty fragrance. Louise resumed her guiding role. "This wood has all been kiln-dried. It's brought in from the outside through that door on the far side of the room," she explained waving a hand as we passed through into the main section of the shop.

Opening out of that middle room was the working shop, complete with a maze of machines and workbenches. Standing by the wood-turning lathe near the front window was a small man with a brown scruffy beard. It was Herman Estes. Later I would learn he had a legendary background. Herman had been born in Kentucky with claims of descent from Daniel Boone. In

World War I he had lied about his age to enlist in the army, had served in Europe, and was proud to be a disabled veteran. He had received injuries from poison gas and had chronic breathing difficulties. Nevertheless, he held a pipe between his teeth almost continually. A wonderful crooked smile lit up his face and crinkled his dark brown eyes. As he removed the pipe with his left hand, I noticed that the crucial fourth finger was missing. He extended a genial right hand, wedding ring there, and shook my hand vigorously.

He cocked his head to one side and pushed his dusty work-stained cap back on his head. With real interest he asked, "How do you think you'll like it here in these mountains? That New York you came from is a big place. I passed through yonder on my way to and from overseas. It sure is a big city." Herman's sense of kinship with me, because we both knew the big city, formed an immediate bond. Few people here had ever experienced as much travel. It was one of his ways of asserting leadership in his role as the one in charge of the woodworking shop.

"I love it here," I told him. "I'd really like to see what you are doing on the lathe and the other machines."

Herman showed me around proudly. He demonstrated a bit on the lathe where he was turning the rungs of a ladder-back chair. Then he pointed out the drill press, the vices, and the hand tools and chisels hanging above the workbenches that lined one wall. Fascinated, I asked if I could learn to turn wood on the lathe. Genially he replied, as he would many times again, "No ma'am, there's not a way in the world a girl could do that."

His discrimination against women outraged the feminism in me, but I didn't question him further that morning. In time Herman taught me never to take his "no's" as the final answer. I genuinely believed all things were possible. As we worked together, I was usually able to convince him that there was a way, in spite of his ready response, "Not a way in the world," to anything unexpected.

This shop also served as a classroom. Here the boys learned woodworking, and "even the girls" did some chip carving, making patterns on the tops of stools and on tiles, trays, and breadboards. We turned from the lathe to the band saw in the center of the room. A tall man in overalls, dusty felt hat pushed back on his thinning hair, turned off the whizzing blade as we approached. "This is Wallace Massey," Herman told me. Wallace and I shook hands. I asked what he was making.

"This here is a carving block," he told me, holding up the piece he had been working on. It was a piece of dark wood, three inches thick, five inches wide, and ten inches long, part of it already cut away. He held it across for me to see. "We mark off the pattern on the wood, and then I saw along the pencil lines to make the block for someone to carve. See, this is a goose block." He pointed out the line on the unfinished piece with his stubby fingernail.

"I can't ever get this black walnut stain off my fingers," he apologized. His skill and patience in using the band saw to fashion blocks for the carvers, hour after hour, day after day, seemed more important to me than unstained hands. I assured him that I didn't believe that the stain mattered when the results of his work made the beautiful carvings possible.

Suddenly I looked around and found that Louise had left the shop. I should probably be back with her. Reluctantly I made my excuses about needing to get to work and left the shop feeling satisfied that here was the source of the supply of materials for the craft department. It would be the lifeline for the finished products I would need as I filled orders in the year ahead. It functioned as a producing heart for the school, and I would make many trips there to take its pulse. It was reassuring to have met the men who made it work.

Back in the office-finishing-shipping room, three young women now sat at the long table by the windows. They were working silently, deftly painting each carving from the pile with a coat of shellac. They then set each napkin ring and animal carefully on its feet to dry. The sharp, pungent odor of the finish filled the room.

Louise took me by the arm, and we walked over to the table. "Girls," she said, "this is Ellie Lambert. She is going to take Fannie Kate Brendle's place and help me here this winter."

She smiled and turned to me. "Ellie, you met Jewell and these are her helpers. Bea is Wallace Massey's wife. You just met him in the woodworking shop. They ride down from Warne together to work here. And here is Louise Coker. She grew up on Little Brasstown and just married Troy Ledford, but he joined the army last month, and she decided to come here to work while he is gone. Louise and Bea are both almost as new to this work as you are. With the enrollment of students down this fall, we were lucky to find them to help out."

All three smiled and bobbed their heads in acknowledgment. Louise had managed to make me feel a sense of team effort and belonging, but the girls never missed a carving, working steadily on. As I returned to the business of packing a small order Louise had assembled for me, they resumed a low murmur of conversation punctuated at times by quiet laughter. A warm atmosphere of good nature pervaded the shop. That feeling was to be a mainstay for me throughout my work there.

A little later that morning we heard the farm pickup truck, with milk cans jiggling together in the back, roar to a stop at the front of the shop. The driver came in quickly without a knock. He looked very boyish in tight pants tucked into tall boots, a broad-brimmed black felt hat pushed back on his smooth brown hair.

"Any packages for the post office?" he asked, grinning at the assembled women. Jewell nodded toward me, as I continued my packing, and asked, "Ellie, have you met *Mon*roe Wilson? He always comes by to pick up packages we want to mail and to bring us empty boxes for packing." I was surprised as I had never heard "Monroe" pronounced that way before.

"Why, no," I said, "we haven't met." I nodded shyly across the room at this man who seemed to have taken us all by storm. He murmured a friendly, self-confident, "Welcome to the Folk School."

Jewell assured him, "We don't have anything ready for you today, Monroe," and he left as quickly as he had appeared.

Louise had gone back over to Keith House, so I decided to take a break and joined the girls at their table. They gave me a short background history of Monroe, a former student who had stayed on in charge of the Folk School dairy. They said that he was the life of every party there, full of energy and laughter, light of foot, and quick with a joke. After my curiosity was satisfied about Monroe and his air of confident ownership, I stayed at the finishing table long enough to get a bit more acquainted with my co-workers.

When I asked them to tell me about themselves, Jewell spoke quietly, "We live right here in Brasstown. My parents are Roxie and Elmer Sales. We did live up on Dog Branch, but the road was not even graveled and always got very muddy in the winter and spring. This year we moved out of the mud. Our new house is close to the store and post office."

"That sounds convenient," I agreed. "Do you have brothers and sisters?"

"Yes, ma'am, two sisters and a brother. I finished high school and came to the Folk School classes last year."

Bea told me that she and Wallace had been married only a short time. "We've known each other all our lives. Our families were neighbors in the Warne community. My mother is a widow, so we're living with her until we can move out on our own."

Louise Coker Ledford was from up the creek a few miles from the school. She spoke so softly I could hardly catch the words. "Troy is going across the water, and I thought this would be the right time to work a little away from home."

It was good to be included in their conversation. I began to feel more relaxed. The girls continued to paint the carvings with sheen coat while we talked. Before I could find something to keep myself busy, Louise came back from Keith House. She greeted me with an invitation, "Would you like to fill in your first day with one more introduction? Murray Martin is working in the weaving room over at Keith House. It would be a good time to meet her and see the gift shop."

I welcomed the chance to get outside and walk back to Keith House, where the gift shop was on the main floor. Two large windows looked out at the tiny village of Brasstown in the near distance. The blue mountain backdrop in the distance gave me a sense of peace, eradicating some of my weariness. While we waited for Murray to finish her work in the next room, Louise and I examined the shelves where carvings were displayed in attractive groups. A small table held handwoven place mats and napkins in carved squirrel rings. On a wooden coat rack near the door were capes woven of vegetable-dyed wool. "This would be a great place to buy gifts to take home," I thought.

As we looked around, Murray Martin came through the door at the back of the room with hand outstretched in greeting. "I'm so glad to meet you," she purred in a soft northern accent. Murray had been an occupational therapist in Baltimore, Maryland, before Mrs. Campbell recruited her to come to the Folk School to teach carving and weaving. I guessed her to be thirty-some, an attractive plump lady who had recently married a former student and made her home on an adjoining farm. "Would you like to see the weaving room as well?" she asked after we had exchanged greetings and pleasantries.

We went into the next room. It was almost filled with looms. Leila Stalcup was busy weaving cloth on a wide loom near the windows. I went to admire the soft rose color of the material. She swayed back and forth on the small bench in front of the loom maintaining a steady rhythm as she passed the shuttle between the warp and woof, beating each thread in place. At another loom, a student was weaving a picture. She had sketched the country scene on the warp threads and was filling in the mountains with short pieces of yarn in autumn hues. A third student was weaving a colorful woolen runner on a nar-row loom. They all looked up and smiled in greeting, but the work continued without interruption. They were readying prod-ucts to be sold to benefit the school at sales "up north" that were held each holiday season outside of Washington, Philadelphia, Boston, and New York.

Soon the gong rang in the dining room below. Louise and I went down to midday dinner and afterward returned to the shop. The girls had taken time off to eat lunches they had brought from home and were back at work. That first day was my initiation into the ritual. Later I came to enjoy the breaks from shop routine: a trip to Keith House to get the mail, a consult with Murray about stock needed, and contact with the carvers of the community; but the pressure of business always took me back to the shop sooner than I liked. Usually we worked until three, taking time out only for dinner at noon.

That first day after Louise and Bea left to catch rides home, and it was time to close shop, Jewell and I swept up. Jewell was adept, but I felt my awkwardness. Having grown up in a carpeted home, I counted on her to demonstrate her technique of working from the sides of the room toward the middle. Then she swept the dust pile neatly onto a flat piece of cardboard and deposited all in the trash barrel.

After tidying up, Jewell and I walked over toward Keith House. We parted in the gravel road and she headed home toward Brasstown down the hill, saying cheerily, "Come and go home with me." I wasn't at all sure how I should respond. Perhaps it would be rude to refuse. It was such a hospitable thing for her to say, and I was tempted to accept. I would have liked being welcomed in someone's home just then. I was still feeling pangs of homesickness. Fortunately I thought better of accepting. Soon after this introduction to mountain graciousness, I learned that this was a colloquial expression and not literally an invitation. It was a customary way of parting, and conveyed the genuine hospitality that is part of rural life.

"Not today, thank you," I replied. "See you tomorrow." With a sense of relief and satisfaction, I headed for my little room at the top of the stairs for a well-deserved rest before supper.

Cherokee County Fair

Doris Ulmann. Photo courtesy of the John C. Campbell Folk School Archives, Brasstown, North Carolina.

"One of the missions of the school was to introduce people to the advantages of good thoroughbred farm stock."

THE AUTUMN AIR became cooler in the weeks that followed. The sky was a brilliant blue, and trees took on their unique leaf colors. The wooded patch behind my workspace in the shop became russet as oak leaves turned. I glimpsed yellow hickories scattered among the oaks. I noticed a few scarlet maples and whole hillsides of golden poplar with the blue mountains in the distance. The color cheered me, and I fell deeply in love with the beauty of the country. I was content with the everyday routines of the large Folk School family, and I began to regain my joy in life as the homesick feelings ebbed.

My enthusiasm at the prospect of a year's work in the mountains of North Carolina had offered a chance to learn more about farming. However, I had not imagined anything as specific as collecting eggs from chickens or milking Jersey cows. Georg Bidstrup pleaded daily for help on the farm. In his heavy Danish accent, he would say, "With so many of the boys signing up for service or going off to verk in the factories, ve need someone to feed the hens and gather the eggs."

In response, I volunteered to feed the chickens and gather the eggs. One hundred New Hampshire red laying hens were housed in a long wooden shed on the slope above Farm House. I loved this contact with the clucking girls after a day of packing, shipping, and billing. Farming was a completely new experience for me and filled a need for which I had longed since childhood. I remembered the pleasure my sister and I had enjoyed when vacationing in Nantucket as little girls and fed chickweed to a neighbor's flock through the holes in their wire enclosure.

One afternoon toward suppertime, I was changing clothes in my little room at the top of the stairs in Keith House when I heard a whooping cry from below. "Yoo-hoo, Ellie, are you up there?" The boys were not allowed to come up the stairs. I peered over the wooden railing.

It was Monroe, that live wire, flirty man about the farm. "Do you want to go in to the fair with me? I need to feed the animals there and bring one of the cows home in the truck."

"Sure," I said, "but what will we do about supper? It's almost time for the bell right now." Never one to skip a meal, my first thought was of my empty stomach.

"Aw, we'll tell them we won't be here, and we'll grab something to eat in town. Come on!" he urged.

"My first date in the mountains!" I thought as I hoisted myself into the dark green pickup truck parked in front of Keith House. The high climb to the slippery, scarred brown leather seat initiated in me a quiet sense of excitement. It was my first ride in a truck of any sort. I tucked my calico broomstick skirt carefully under my knees and hung on to the seat with both hands as we swung around a sharp curve down the narrow, gravel road. We turned left on U.S. Highway 64 toward Murphy, and I relaxed a bit as the old, black macadam smoothed the bumps to a gentle roll.

With a sense of small adventure at playing hooky from the usual structure of a Folk School evening, we laughed and joked and made plans. We would enjoy the midway after we had taken care of the school's farm animals and examined the displays of vegetables, fruit, jams, jellies, home-baked goodies, and handicrafts from the farms and homes in the county. Monroe promised solemnly, "The midway with hot dogs, cotton candy, rides on the Ferris wheel, and booths to test our skill will crown the evening."

As we drove over the bridge and out of Clay County, Monroe took on his role as tour guide. "This is Peachtree. On your left you will see the prison camp." He waved his hand toward high barbed wire fences surrounding low whitewashed barracks. "It's really exciting around here when they have a breakout," he teased.

"What kinds of prisoners are there?" I asked.

"Almost any kind of crime," he began, but glanced at my face and modified his tale into "nothing very desperate, mostly robbery, I guess." He laughed. "It is exciting, though, when the sirens go off, and the guards start hunting with bloodhounds."

I knew he was teasing and settled back, enjoying the broad farming valley where Peachtree Creek runs into the Hiwassee River. Farther on, the road wound between the smooth upland river and the rock-hewn mountain. As we topped Scott Laney Mountain, I glanced at the small river bottom way below. I remembered that this was the very spot where, last spring, my roommate Peg claimed driving dizziness, and Liz had taken over. It had been foggy then, obscuring the depth of the valley below. Now I smiled at the innocence of the climb. I glanced quickly at my date, who held the steering wheel in the easy fashion of one for whom mountain driving was second nature.

The road to the county seat was familiar. Passing the beautiful marble courthouse, we skirted the town square with its fountain and the stone watering troughs. Passing the First Methodist Church, which faced the end of Valley River Avenue, we headed for the fair grounds across the Valley River Bridge.

The Cherokee County Fair was a big event in the years before World War II. It took place along the Valley River below the Murphy schools. The exhibits were in the old Rock Gym. Behind it were the pens and sheds for the animals and a small sawdust ring for showing before the judges' stand. In front of the gym and stretching to the river on one side and to the macadam road toward Andrews on the far end was the colorful midway brought in from out of town.

The Folk School was showing a well-built Jersey cow named Mabel. One of the missions of the school was to introduce people to the advantages of good thoroughbred farm stock in order to improve milk supply and standards of living in the country. I could hardly wait to see what blue ribbons the school would collect. Then the sound of the calliope and the lights beginning to come on across the midway caught my attention. A strange sense of unreality touched me. This was all so far removed from life in New York. I was a completely different person.

Monroe parked the truck behind the gym near the entrance to the animal quarters and helped me down. Hand-in-hand, we walked to the gate, where he showed his pass. Turning to the right, we threaded our way on sawdust paths between sheds and cages. The heavy feathery odor of chickens and the ammonia-sharp fumes from their droppings assailed my nose. Cackling came from several directions, occasionally punctuated by the raucous crow of a rooster. Although in my new role as poultry woman at the school I wanted to compare the Rhode Island reds on display with the white Leghorns, we hurried by. I had to postpone my chicken research due to the urgency of caring for the cow.

I contented myself by glancing quickly at the many varieties of caged birds as we passed. A few triangular wooden cages of colorful lean roosters prompted me to ask curiously, "What are these?" The quick dismissing reply of "fighting roosters" did not encourage further examination. I realized some time later that the sport of fighting cocks was illegal in this country, but the business of raising these birds to ship overseas brought in welcome cash.

In the distance, we could hear the stomping and neighing of horses. I was surprised to notice that I could distinguish the fresh scent of horse manure from the sweet cow piles in the straw-bedded stalls of the cattle. Monroe led purposefully past all these distracting sounds and smells to the cowsheds. Then he stopped so suddenly that I almost bumped into him. He laughed and turned toward me. "Ellie, I want you to meet Mabel. She is the lady we came in to visit. Please notice the beautiful blue ribbon hanging around her pretty neck. They must have completed the judging this afternoon. I thought we were going to get here in time to see it, but never mind, we have better things to do." He stroked her nose affectionately. "Good girl," he said, obviously filled with pride and delight.

I shared his pleasure and reached up to stoke her warm brown neck. "She's beautiful, Monroe," I murmured.

"I'd better milk her before we look around," he said and pulled a small stool and a bucket from the corner of the stall. He poured feed into the trough in front of the cow. Then rolling up the sleeves of his starched white shirt, he sat down and with rhythmic smooth downward massages streamed the milk into the bucket. I leaned over the low fence and watched with fascination. He accomplished the task with amazing speed. Then he stood up quickly and poured the fresh milk into the far corner of the pen to disappear into the straw floor covering.

My thrifty Yankee upbringing caused me to exclaim in horror, "Why did you do that?"

He looked at me in amazement. "We couldn't keep it, milked in this dirty stall, and Mabel had to be tended to tonight."

"Oh." I replied meekly. Monroe set the bucket upside down in the corner of the pen, opened the gate, and joined me in the hallway between stalls. We wandered around peering over fences and looking through bars. Placards on the outside of each pen displayed the animals' names and the owners' names and addresses. We stopped, looking for other Folk School entries.

"This is Gladys," Monroe introduced, bowing in mock formality. "She's not quite a year old, and we thought she'd have as good a judging as Mabel, but she has a white ribbon at least."

"It's all right, Gladys," I consoled. "It'll be your turn next time. You're beautiful too."

My guide recognized a few more animal acquaintances, including some from McComb's dairy herd in Peachtree. Then we came to a section of larger pens. We paused in front of a large Jersey bull with some black markings on his smooth brown coat. "Now this is the Mister," Monroe introduced proudly. "We'll just leave him alone."

I made no comment. We had seen enough of the livestock, and laughing, we proceeded to the Rock Gym. The large hall was crowded with a variety of people drawn together by a common interest in the harvest. All ages, shapes, and sizes of curious spectators mingled in an excited throng.

In the bleachers on both sides of the gym were displays of home crafts. Colorful quilts, crocheted tablecloths, and bedspreads stretched out along the top row. Embroidered towels and dishcloths, and crocheted doilies, stiff with sugar starch, were arranged on tables below. Among the displays of clothing, most of the children's dresses and pajamas were made of printed material that had originally been sacks holding chicken feed. Every kind of apron hung proudly from a tightly strung clothesline. Styles ranging from copious coveralls with bibs and pockets to dainty lace-trimmed party styles competed for the blue, red, white, and green ribbons, which designated winners. A large gold seal with a fluted blue ribbon designated the grand prizewinner.

Children ducked in and out of the crowd. Women were predominantly curious, stopping to examine work they particularly admired, often with an eye to copying it themselves at home. Eagerly they sought out their own entries and, hearts beating anxiously, hoped for a prize ribbon and the cash award that accompanied it at the end.

Near the bleacher displays were the club entries. Four-H clubs, Home Demonstration Clubs, civic groups, and some churches competed for best group display. Each graphically showed the purpose and achievements of the organization. For example, the 4-H exhibit showed head, hands, heart, and health, each on a large poster with photographs of young people accomplishing prizewinning projects in each category.

After a while Monroe told me, "I just want to wander around outside. I'll be watching for you at the entrance to the midway. Just take your time and look it all over."

In the center of the room were long tables holding every variety of farm produce. There were rows of huge orange pumpkins and all kinds of winter squash: acorn, Hubbard, butternut, and even some late, yellow crookneck summer squash. Next were the gourds: long-handled, round, smooth-colored, and spotted in shades of dark green, orange, and white. I had never seen gourds before, and I asked the older lady standing next to me, "What are they good for?" She didn't understand the question, and I had to rephrase it. "What do you use those for? Can you eat them?"

She laughed pleasantly. "Why lawsy no, Hon. They're just to use or for show. Some old folks use those long-handled ones to dip water. Where do you come from?" I was embarrassed and made some excuse to move on to the tables covered with home-canned goods, not willing to disclose my urban Yankee upbringing.

The jams and jellies shone. Glass jars held watermelon and okra pickles, and pickled corn and beans, in addition to the dill and bread-and-butter cucumber pickles I knew so well. Vegetables for the winter shared space with baked goods, cakes, pies, and biscuits. They made me hungry, so I slipped out the big, wide doors and found the entrance to the midway. Monroe was standing beside the Lions Club refreshment pavilion. He saw me coming and greeted me with a hot dog in each hand. "What do you want to drink?" he asked.

We each bought a carton of milk and, refreshments in hand, headed for the Ferris wheel. He bought the tickets, and we chose a seat. The music started and we lifted off, rising gently until, section by section, all the seats were full. At the top, the wheel stopped. Our seat swung back and forth. Monroe stretched his arm across the back of our seat protectively. The view from the top was spectacular, as the lights of Murphy faded in the background of the fully illuminated midway.

What an evening that was! We hardly missed a trick. Monroe demonstrated his sharpshooting skill as I admired. He won a hideous plush dog and gave it to me to carry. We gambled shamefully with the penny toss. He was successful, but I quickly became bored. We avoided the sideshows of the Fat Lady, the monster, and some freak animals with two heads, but we rode the merry-go-round, the bumper cars, and everything else until we were dizzy. Finally it was time to go home. Proprietors were closing the booths by letting down canvas covers and securing them at each side. The crowd was moving slowly toward the exit.

I waited while Monroe found the truck. He backed it to the gate, and I helped him load a reluctant Mabel into the straw-filled bed and lock the tailgate. Satisfied with a successful evening, we headed for Brasstown.

We hadn't lacked for conversation since we had set out that night, but finally as we headed for home we began to get personally acquainted by sharing information about our homes, his in rural north Georgia, mine in suburban New York. Swapping tales, he told me about helping his Uncle Luther truck farm produce to Atlanta the summer of his last year in high school. As he drove, he ran his free hand through his thick, brown hair to draw it back from his forehead.

"Do you look like your dad?" I asked.

"No," he replied, "my Dad was bald, but he died two years ago."

"I'm sorry to hear that," I said, somewhat embarrassed. "Do you have a big family?"

"Dad left Mother with my two teenage brothers to raise."

"Do you have any sisters?" I asked.

He laughed, and that mischievous smile showed in the lights as we passed the prison camp in Peachtree. "Yes," he said, "six."

"You're joking," I exclaimed. "Nobody has six sisters!"

"Oh yes, I do."

"Name them."

"Well," he stuttered, "let me see. There's Myrtle and Bessie and um—"

"I know you're teasing. You couldn't have six sisters all older than you."

"No Maggie is younger, but she's married."

"Is that her real name?"

"No, it's Magdalene, after my Grandmother Wilson."

"Well," I said, somewhat mollified by this morsel of fact, "what are the others' names?"

"There's Annie Mae, and Caledonia, and Jerry, I think," he clowned.

"Now I know you're joking. You said you had a brother named Jerry. You can't have a brother and a sister with the same names!" I laughed.

He laughed too and said his brother's real name was Jarrell. We left it at that, but it was some time before I believed that he really did have six sisters and three brothers. We laughed all the way back to Keith House, where I thanked him and said good night as he headed for the barn and his own apartment in Tower House. It was good to have a friend close to my own age and to have some sense of life beyond the Folk School.

A Visit to
Downtown Brasstown

"Fred O. sat on a high stool behind the counter."

SOON ANOTHER OPPORTUNITY to explore wider horizons came my way. The Folk School owned a sedate four-door Chevrolet as well as the farm truck in which we had gone to the fair. Louise used the blue car frequently and kept it in the garage at Farm House, but it was also available for other staff members to use on school business. One day not long after I arrived, Louise asked, "Ellie, do you drive?"

Actually, I had never managed to get a driver's license although I had dearly wanted one. Only that past summer, my mother had been able to relinquish her fears enough to allow me to take the wheel. So I was able to assure Louise truthfully, "Yes, I drove the family car in Maine this summer, but no license is required there."

"I'll go with you today while you try out the blue car. We need to introduce you to Mrs. Green at the post office. You should be able to take the packages over in the afternoon and pick up the second mail of the day, then we'll go to Murphy to secure a North Carolina license for you. All that is required here is a small fee and a statement from a reliable friend that you are capable of driving."

The next morning I packed orders with a new sense of excitement. I weighed, labeled, stamped, and insured each box. At the post office, Mrs. Iowa Green would sack them, and the mail truck would pick them up for the trip to Gainesville, Georgia, which was the nearest postal collection point for the railroad.

About two o'clock, Louise brought the car over from Keith House and helped me load the packages in the trunk and on the back seat. A bit nervously, I took the driver's seat and looked over the different knobs and pedals. Gripping the steering wheel tightly, I pushed in the clutch and shifted into low gear. We jerked forward, but Louise didn't even gasp. As I tried to coordinate gas pedal and clutch, we bucked our way down the gravel road toward Brasstown. Out of the corner of my eye, I was aware that Louise was sitting on the edge of her seat, but she didn't say a word.

Where the gravel road reached the paved U.S. Highway 64, we stopped. There was a small general store on the left. Louise said, "Let's go in. I'd like for you to meet Quedor Caldwell. Quedor married Lillian Scroggs, and they have five little ones now. Quedor is a fine storekeeper; everyone likes to trade with him. Sometimes he takes his truck and goes down to Atlanta for a load of really fresh produce."

The store had no large storefront window, so the inside was not brightly lit. In other ways it was a lot like country stores I had known in Maine. Quedor Caldwell was a slim man with a soiled tan fedora hat pushed back on his head. He stepped forward and offered his hand in the manner of a host, welcoming us as we went in. He had a fetching smile and good manners. His wife stood behind the counter that held a glass case full of penny candy. Lillian had a quiet dignity befitting her role in a family that had lived in Brasstown for many years. A striped apron enveloped her thickened body. A Coca-Cola cooler stood next to the counter, its top open for all to see the bottles on ice.

Louise introduced me all around, even to the small group of customers standing about. I nodded and smiled. While Louise continued with friendly greetings, my eyes roved along the shelves. I noticed Southern products not yet part of my experience: grits in boxes, pinto beans in cans, and a bin of yams over by a potbellied stove in the center of the store. Then Louise said we must go on to the post office.

I resumed the driver's seat and turned the car right on U.S. Highway 64. Mercifully, the paving made it easier for me to maintain an even pace. Going a block, we reached the second and third general stores that made up the town of Brasstown. We turned left between the two stores, onto another gravel road, and traveled about five hundred yards to the tiny post office on the edge of a field. Mrs. Iowa Green had the small structure erected for herself after she was appointed postmistress of Brasstown, a position of some prominence that widows in small communities often held before the institution of Social Security.

The post office was a tiny weathered building. A small round sign indicated its status as a U.S. Postal Service facility. I estimated it to be about ten feet wide and perhaps twelve feet deep. Short rough logs on end functioned as wooden stilts to level the building off the ground at the back. We entered the lobby through a wooden door that creaked as it swung open into a narrow space, two feet deep. The lobby extended across the ten-foot front of the building. A small frame window beside the front door admitted a bit of light. The walls were posted with notices of rewards offered for information on the whereabouts of criminals wanted for theft, murder, or petty misdeeds. Elsewhere in the lobby, other important information about schedules, rates, and regulations was posted in every available space so that there was ample reading material if a line of waiting customers was able to squeeze into the area.

Mrs. Green lifted a wooden window in the center of a rough board counter to welcome us as she heard the front door open. She secured the opening by placing a stick prop under the shutter to hold it up. Leaning on the counter on her side of the opening, she greeted us. "Good afternoon. Lawsy, it is good to see you, Louise. Is this your new helper?"

"This is Ellie Lambert, Iowa. She is taking Fannie Kate Brendle's place in the shop, now that Fannie Kate is going to Washington, D.C., to work."

"Pleased to meet you." Mrs. Green bobbed her head in an obsequious gesture as if in deference to our status. The Folk School was the biggest patron of the Brasstown post office and had been influential in having Iowa Green appointed post-mistress. Cordially she invited us to come around. "If you don't mind I'll have to close the window now. Would you please bring the packages around to the side door? Then I can get them sacked up before the mail truck comes. I'd like to show you the office."

She closed the window. We left the lobby and walked around to the side door as she flung it open hospitably. Mrs. Green was a small woman, dressed neatly with a large apron completely covering her black skirt and flower-printed shirtwaist. She shook hands with each of us. Louise went inside with her, and I turned to unload the trunk and the back seat of the car, which was piled high with packages.

The interior of the post office was a small room, barely ten feet square. A single light bulb reached down from a wire and lighted a long table on the wall opposite us. It was cleared in readiness for the incoming mail to be spilled from the pouches and sorted. Several rows of cubicles hung above the counter to hold letters addressed to go out on the rural route in the morning. Next to the service window were twenty or thirty small cubicles for the mail of local patrons who lived close to the heart of "downtown" Brasstown. They usually picked up their mail as soon as the window was opened after the carrier truck left. People gathered to see each other and get the latest news as well as whatever gossip might be there for the gleaning. In those years before rural telephones and radios were common here and television was unknown, the post office was another place to socialize. Although the Folk School mail was delivered each morning on Mr. Vic Bell's rural route, the school usually checked again in the afternoon when we had packages to mail.

Motioning to two high gray stools, Mrs. Green invited us to sit while she examined the boxes and put them in large canvas sacks. As she worked, she kept up a stream of information about the routine at the post office. "Vic Bell will be back in a little while. He's running a bit late today." Turning to me, she explained, "He's our rural carrier, you know. He used to ride horseback on the route until just a few years back, but the roads are better now and he can get around more easily in his Model-A Ford."

As I listened, my eyes went to Mrs. Green's unique filing system. On the wooden wall at the back of the office, charts were skewered up on ten-penny nails, each sharpened to a point to remove the head and make it into a spindle. There was one chart of postal zones, another for the weight charges on packages being mailed to different areas, and a number of pages of official government rules and regulations. On regular nails near the service window, curious paper stubs hung in some random fashion. I asked about them.

"Those are money order stubs. People buy postal orders to pay bills, to order goods by mail, or to send money to their folks elsewhere. It's handy and saves the trouble of having a bank account. Those are their receipts. I keep them there in case they're needed. Sometimes I take in a good bit of money, and regulations say I can't keep more than a hundred dollars here in my cash box. If I take in more I need to send it off by registered mail when the truck comes. I'm afraid something will happen to it, so I keep it with me when I go home. Every noon I go up the road to fix dinner for my mother and my brother Wade. I take my satchel with the cash box and the stamps with me. I'm very careful with the money," she explained.

Mrs. Green was proud of her position as postmistress, and her pride was imbued with the weight of responsibility in caring for so great a trust. It was as if the long arm of the government had put its hand on her shoulder and entrusted its communication system to her personally. On shelves under the table and service counter, she kept the *Manual of Instruction*, her book of wax paper pages separating the sheets of stamps of each denomination, and other business and personal items. I felt important and privileged to see the entire operation of the post office that afternoon.

After we had been at the post office for almost an hour, the mail truck from Gainesville, Georgia, was due to arrive. Vic Bell had not yet returned from his route, but Louise said we needed to move on. As we climbed into the car, she confided, "We were going to stop for a minute at the Scroggs's General Store on our way back. I wanted you to meet Mr. Fred O., but it will have to wait for another day. I'm afraid we stayed too long at the post office."

The next day Louise drove me into Murphy with her hand firmly in control of the car. At the square, we turned right and parked along Valley River Avenue. We went through a plain unmarked door between two stores. Up a steep narrow staircase, we found a small office over a dress shop. Inside there was a long table under a window that looked out on the main street. The examiner for auto vehicle licenses was working on a pile of applications. He looked up as we came in, and Louise introduced me. In his most informal and friendly way he asked polite questions about my age, birthplace, how I happened to be in North Carolina, and how much experience I had with driving. He filled out my application, asked me to sign it, and gave me a North Carolina driver's license.

It became my daily task to visit Mrs. Green at the post office. Some afternoons she asked me to explain letters she received from the Post Office Department in Washington. The government had a way of making a simple statement sound very confusing, and I was able to translate it in simple terms. She was most appreciative. I heard about her family. Here at home she had her mother, Granny Beach, who was blind and nearing a hundred years of age. Mrs. Green's unmarried brother, Wade, lived with them also. Son Worth was away, working in Atlanta, and daughter Opal was finishing her senior year at Berea College in Kentucky.

Mrs. Green was proud of her family. As often as they were able, they attended Hickory Stand Methodist Church, just up Green Cove Road from her home. Gradually I was able to learn the news of the community. There was no one Mrs. Green didn't know, and she was willing to tell me anything I wanted to know about Brasstown. Her simple honesty and devotion to work and family impressed me, and I loved her egalitarian spirit and sense of community. Country living was so personally rooted. It was a wonderful change for me from the distancing I had experienced in suburbia and the impersonal atmosphere of the big city. I was anxious to know everyone and to see more of the community.

Soon after my introduction to the post office, Louise and I formed the habit of visiting people in Brasstown almost weekly. That year Mr. Fred O. Scroggs had rented his store on the corner to Mr. and Mrs. Bass Duval. They were longtime storekeepers from Warne, who wanted to extend their business to Brasstown.

Fred O. was a good wheeler and dealer so he moved out of his big store and collected rent on it while he remodeled the smaller building across the side street and maintained his business there. The architecture of his remodeled business was interesting. There was one room in front and a two-story addition on the back. We went in under a long store sign stretched across the front of the building. Inside it was dark and smoky, heavy with the odor of tobacco. Men were smoking cigarettes and pipes and chewing, their jaws puffed out and lips pressed tightly together. On shelves around the room and on display in glass cases were all kinds of tobacco products: cigarettes, pipe tobacco, loose tobacco and papers for "rolling your own," plugs of tobacco to chew, cigars, and many brands of snuff in small cans and boxes. Men were lounging around the room. As we entered, some who had been seated in straight-backed chairs, leaning back against the wall, deftly tilted them forward on all four legs and stood awkwardly grouped as if misery loved company.

Two-thirds of the way back in the room, a counter divided the store from a smaller room, which showed through an open door in the middle of the back wall. Fred O. sat on a high stool behind the counter. His head rested on his left hand, his arm propped on one elbow. He was laying forth facts in a genial fashion to the group of men gathered attentively around him. As we came in, a hush fell over the store. Fred O. stood up to welcome us. Louise introduced me as her new helper from New York City, and we shook hands across the counter. I could see Fred O. sizing me up with keen brown eyes in a tanned leathery face, a faint smile creasing his dark lips. I wondered what he thought of me.

These men were the power brokers of Brasstown, and we had interrupted a male caucus. Even the side exchanges of earthy jokes and the latest gossip ebbed away as we intruded. I looked around at the wall shelves holding boxes and cans of staples. Crackers and a few loaves of "light bread" stood on the counter. A musty odor blended with the scent of tobacco. We exchanged observations about the weather while Louise bought some crackers. Several men reached forth and shook my hand in a reticent grandfatherly fashion that I found charmingly courteous and welcoming. One tall fellow asked me, "Who are you kin to, Miss?"

"No one around here, sir," I replied, and the incredulous disappointment and murmur of amusement surprised me. I felt intimidated by this encounter with the men of the community, but I was curious to learn more about them. I responded to the chorus of "Come back, y'all," with a shy smile and a quiet "thank you" as we left.

Next, Louise and I went to see Granny Lillie Scroggs. She lived on the hill directly across from the gravel road that led to the Folk School. Her house was built in the mountain style of some early country homes that were larger than the log cabins.

It commanded a view of both the Little Brasstown and the Hiwassee River valleys. A generous front porch facing a large magnolia tree welcomed people to the house. In a huge pot on the porch was a very old Christmas cactus. Granny was proud of it, and I took her picture. The kitchen ell included a back porch enclosing the well. This was a forerunner to the convenience of a sink in the kitchen. It saved many a trip out in the weather to draw water.

On our first visit, Granny Scroggs told me in her deep voice, "The old road to Murphy went right by this house. It was rough, but then everyone traveled by horse and wagon. For a number of years this house served as a post office and provided a place for wagons and mail carriers to rest." Granny's parents were among early settlers in Clay County and are buried in the little family cemetery on the hill across from her house. Granny was Lillie Strange before she married Luce Scroggs. They raised six children on their place. She was proud that her husband and her son Fred O. had encouraged Marguerite Butler and Olive Campbell to locate the Folk School in Brasstown. They had generously given land to get the school established.

Granny told me about their six children. Their eldest son, Fred O., had chosen to go to college in Young Harris, Georgia, and became the storekeeper in Brasstown. When Miss Marguerite Butler first stopped at his store in 1925 to ask about the availability of land in the area, Fred O. saw an opportunity to locate a school here. At that time the community had been disappointed that the new elementary school for the western part of the county was located at Ogden, halfway between Brasstown and Warne, instead of here in the Brasstown community. Fred O. liked the Folk School dream of a school for everyone who wanted to learn, rather than a school for "teachers and preachers." He was delighted when Mrs. Campbell saw the "loafers' bench" at his store and recognized the fact that many carvers in the community could turn their talent into a profitable business.

Granny said that after Luce Scroggs died, she divided the land among their children. Although several in the family sold their land and moved away in search of better opportunities elsewhere, Fred O., Jim, Lillian, and a large number of grandchildren were still here. Fred and Lillian were storekeepers, and Jim was a farmer and cattle trader.

Another afternoon Louise and I drove up Green Cove Road to the John Brendle house. We needed to return a beautiful wall hanging that the Brendles' daughter, Fannie Kate, had woven at the Folk School. First she had sketched the mountains in an art class taught by June Cary. Then she had copied the sketch on one of the large looms at Keith House. Finally, she had woven the picture in a medley of russet and lavender. It was beautifully done, framed simply in black walnut.

Fannie Kate was home that afternoon, but she planned to leave the next day for her new job in Washington, D.C. I was glad to meet her before she left. She was little older than I, poised and gracious in telling me of her experience in working with Louise in the craft department, and wishing me well. In turn I shared with her some of my experiences with friends in Washington during my school and college years. Fannie Kate was as excited about exploring new opportunities as was I.

On the way back down Green Cove Road, we turned at a deserted old Methodist Church and drove across a broad open field to the house Harriet and Gwen Cornwell were building on the land they had bought from Carl Scroggs, another of Granny's sons who had gone to Asheville. We had promised Harriet before we left Keith House that afternoon that we would check on the progress they were making on their home. The house was on the side of the hill just above the collection of stores in Brasstown and across from the Scroggs's hill. The ground was so rocky that they had dynamited a deep hole in order to place a full basement under the frame house.

Louise parked the car up beside a quaint old barn. We walked down to the house and across a plank that bridged the opening to a tiny, screened porch outside the room that would be Gwen's farm office. He was planning to have a chicken hatchery with electric incubators in the basement. With pride he showed us the roughed-in rooms and asked us to come back later when Harriet would be home from work and could tell us more about their vision for the future. This was my first visit to one of the homes of a Folk School couple in Brasstown. There were five or six farms already established and more to come as the school planned to encourage the development of the community in the years ahead.

One Sunday afternoon, we walked cross-country up the gentle valley formed by Little Brasstown Creek. There was a singing up there at Maggie's Chapel, and a group of the girls wanted to go to the event with Louise, so I went along too. After the service and singing, we walked back toward the Folk School on the narrow gravel road that led to Brasstown. It was so warm that I took off my shoes to walk barefoot. The girls walked on ahead, but Louise stopped me, saying, "You shouldn't go without your shoes here. This isn't like New England. There's a real danger of getting hookworm if you walk barefoot." I was surprised and a little chagrined, but I put my shoes back on. Soon a neighbor from the Martin's Creek Community stopped his car and offered us a ride back to the school. It was an offer Louise and I couldn't refuse, so we climbed in thankfully. Two other passengers, Doc Teems and Will Mason, were also catching a ride to Brasstown, and Louise introduced me. Again, I was asked, "Who are you kin to?" and they were surprised that I had no relatives in the mountains. Family was very important, and I felt a bit strange not to be able to identify with anyone they knew.

However, with each of our visits into the surrounding countryside, I became a bit more familiar with the unique life in the mountains of Western North Carolina. Gradually I began to feel more at home.

🌿 *Chatuge Dam:* 🌿
Change in the Air

Doris Ulmann. Photo courtesy of the John C. Campbell Folk School Archives, Brasstown, North Carolina.

"Georg enjoyed teasing me about Vassar."

DESPITE THE FRIENDLY WELCOMES and Louise's introductions, sometimes I still felt lonely at the Folk School. Certainly, life in the country was very different from my intellectual and social life in college. My childhood in the suburbs of New York City had not prepared me for the freedom of homes widely spaced along rural roads. I gazed around me at the beauty of the purple mountains and marveled at the wondrously different lifestyle that resulted from isolation. I was amazed at the determination of the pioneers, who had braved the thick forests, mazes of rhododendron, rocky cliffs, and tumbling rivers to settle on steep hills and in narrow valleys.

Even now, transportation was not easy. The usual way to travel away from home was by train or bus. If a car was available, the trip was still arduous. The narrow two-lane macadam roads connected towns and wandered through the main street of each small community they reached. A distance of a hundred and fifty miles was a five-hour journey. Unless family or health needs demanded a trip, many people preferred to stay at home.

At the Folk School, students and staff alike politely asked questions about my family, about New York City, and about college. It seemed impossible to describe my thoughts, friends, and family to people who had rarely been to a big city and had no firsthand experience with even Atlanta, Asheville, or Chattanooga.

As we chatted at work in the shop, Jewell told me that some of her high school friends had gone to Atlanta to work for the Bell Telephone Company. "When they come back sometimes for a weekend, they have wonderful stories to tell about how big it is. I wouldn't like it at all. It would be hard to get to know anybody; here I've known everybody all my life."

I found it easier not to explain and describe places that had been home to me. I felt so far from home that I was uncertain of what I could assume to be common knowledge. Certainly, the courses I had taken in college were inexplicable here. I had wrestled with the resolution of conflict between advertising and freedom of the press. Questions about Christianity, social justice, and the meaning of life concerned me, but there was no one with whom I could discuss these issues. Although a part of me missed my former life, there was a freedom for me at the Folk School to leave the past behind in order to explore new ways of living and of being.

Georg enjoyed teasing me about Vassar. An article had appeared not long before in *Life* magazine depicting my college as if it were a finishing school for the wealthy. Georg was somehow delighted to be able to picture his wife in that setting and liked to see me in the same light. However, twenty years had separated our college experiences, and I assured him that during the Depression at least three-quarters of the girls worked their way through college, and that most would go on to become professionals. He doubted my perceptions, but accepted them nonetheless. Recognition as a working member of the Folk School family was important to me. I wanted to shed the mystique of the intellectual world of privilege and to be accepted for myself.

On the other hand, I had to laugh when, for example, Peavine or some other student asked me if I knew a friend of theirs who had recently spent some time at the Brooklyn Navy Yard in service. The implication that coming from New York City meant knowing everyone else there amused me. Attempts to bridge the gulf between the culture in which I had grown up and the life I was now living in Appalachia seemed futile. The distance between the impersonality of big city life and the friendliness of rural society was amazingly clear. Because it was difficult to describe them, I said little about my family or college life.

Gregarious Kentuckian Herman Estes was more at ease with my strangeness because of his visit to New York many years earlier when he was in the army during World War I. He extended a warm welcome to visit with his family. They lived on school property, in the white frame house at the end of the Folk School driveway. One day after work, I walked out to visit and get acquainted with his family.

I found Mabel, Herman's wife, in the yard, scattering corn for her chickens. She was gruff and short-spoken, but ever ready for company. She was glad to tell me about her life. We sat on straight chairs in the yard and visited while she recounted proudly, "Yes, I milk the cow myself; churn the cream into butter; and sell it, along with our extra milk and cream, and fresh eggs to friends in Murphy. We keep our chickens for eggs and meat, and fatten a hog every year. We also have a good garden, and I can all the vegetables and fruit, meat, pickles, and jam we need." Rather than buy bread at the store, Mabel made biscuits and corn bread every day. Sometimes if she sold butter and eggs in Murphy, she had a little spending money of her own. Her first-hand accounts of country self-sufficiency gave me a glimpse of the independence of rural life.

I didn't know much about keeping house or being a wife and mother, so I think I had more in common with the three little Estes girls (Doodle, Dick, and Helen) than with their mother. The children soon came walking down the road from the bus stop at the Folk School. They were tanned and pigtailed, with beautiful dark hair and big brown eyes. They could tell tall tales almost as well as their daddy, and I loved to listen to them. Although I wasn't always sure of all the expressions they used, the cadences and lilt of the stories fascinated me, and we often joined in spontaneous laughter as I took my cues from their expressive faces.

One day at work, Herman asked me out to their house for supper. We sat around a big table in the kitchen. Herman returned thanks to God for the day and for the meal, then he and Mabel piled our plates high with green beans, mashed potatoes and gravy, squash, and fried rabbit. They passed the biscuits, corn bread, butter, and honey in the comb from Herman's own bees. He had shot the rabbit the day before in the field out from their house. Herman prided himself on being a descendent of Daniel Boone and was a skilled hunter and fisherman. We were enjoying the meal, my introduction to wild game, when little Helen, age six, commented, "Do you see how fast this rabbit was running when Daddy shot him? This leg I'm eating is stretched out as far as it will go. He was trying so hard to get away."

Herman and Mabel both admonished her to hush, and the two older girls giggled with embarrassment, but I thought her observation was funny and assured them I wouldn't lose my appetite just thinking about the poor rabbit's former life. After supper Mabel showed me some of her antiques. A tall walnut bed with a steep, high headboard graced Doodle's room. Herman had converted a number of old lamps to electricity. He had also built much of their furniture, including a beautiful corner china cabinet of wild cherry wood, burnished to a glowing shine. We played a game of cards after the show and tell. That evening I walked back to Keith House comforted by a taste of home.

Herman invited me to go with the family to Hayesville one Saturday afternoon. They were going to see the dam the Tennessee Valley Authority was building up there. The dam would end the flooding of the Hiwassee River and store water to generate hydroelectric power. The dam, located in Hayesville, would create a lake on the border between Georgia and North Carolina. The impending threat of war had sped up the construction, and the decision as to its location finally put an end to the rumors that had circulated and to the games those rumors had initiated. At first when the location of this dam was in question, the valley around Peachtree Creek had been surveyed. Then the TVA had considered the land on both sides of Big and Little Brasstown creeks. Rumors were rife. One of the amusements of the time was to spread false information just to see how far the story would travel by word of mouth. Someone would tell a piece of so-called news at a country store in Hayesville one day, the next day the "news" would be repeated at Anderson's store in Warne, and the third or fourth day it would be fact in Brasstown.

There had been a serious flood of the Hiwassee River just east of Murphy in 1940, and it was imperative that the water be brought under control. A dam was being built several miles downriver from Murphy, along with a temporary village for workers, which was named Hiwassee Dam. However, the dam was not sufficient to control the entire course of the river. When the Brasstown community and the Folk School staff heard that there was a possibility the dam would be built at the junction of the Brasstown Creek and the Hiwassee River, they realized that all the farmland in Brasstown would be flooded. Mrs. Campbell contacted David Lilienthal, president of the TVA Board in Knoxville. He assured her that such was not the case, but rumors continued to fly. Finally, the location of the dam was announced. Fourteen thousand acres of land in Clay County, North Carolina, and Towns County, Georgia, were cleared; and work on the Chatuge Dam was begun.

On one bright Saturday afternoon in October, we piled into Herman's chocolate brown car and set out on the road that wound up Big Brasstown Creek toward Warne, the next post office community on the road to Hayesville. U.S. Highway 64 wound across all of North Carolina from the coast to the Tennessee line, but it was narrow and lightly used in the mountains. Herman was a good tour guide as we traveled from Brasstown toward Hayesville. When we passed a rock building and a cluster of other buildings in the Brasstown community, he spoke up. "That's the Mountain Valley Cooperative Creamery and Credit Union. They bottle and market the milk and eggs from the school and from a number of small farms." Farther along, passing a curve, he pointed up a narrow dirt road bridged across the creek and told me, "That leads to the Pine Log Community, where a good number of the carvers you see on Wednesdays live."

The road we followed was sparsely dotted with small houses, surrounded by large garden patches, tiny wire-enclosed chicken lots, cow sheds with fenced pastures, and pigsties. We passed the white wood-framed elementary school at Ogden, and two or three large farms stretched out in open expanses between ridges of hills. Then we arrived in Warne. At the road that branched off to lead toward north Georgia, we stopped at the gas pumps of a country store.

"I need to get some gas before we can go all the way up to the dam," Herman explained, getting out slowly from behind the steering wheel. Mabel sat stolidly staring ahead, and the girls hung out the left back window, begging for this or that: gum, candy, or a Dr. Pepper. Herman hushed them abruptly and rounded the car to my rear window. I had rolled it down as far as it would go to catch whatever breeze might blow that hot October day. I sensed what he wanted because the Folk School staff usually expected anyone who went on a trip to pay expenses. I reached in the pocket of my skirt and asked how much gas we'd need.

"Two dollars will do it," he replied, holding out the callused, brown hand with the fourth finger missing. "That will be about six gallons—enough to get us there and back."

He disappeared into the store and came out with the proprietor, whose dusty straw hat, pushed back on his head, covered a work-worn face and laugh-creased lines around his eyes. He extended a welcoming hand.

"Howdy, miss. I reckon you've come all the way from New York City to see our dam. I hope you'll enjoy the sight," he greeted jovially. He put the six gallons in the tank and bid us good day, "come back, y'all."

We traveled on, passing a few more farmhouses in the Blair Creek valley, surrounded by comfortable hills. On the right, a small white church that Herman identified as Mount Pisgah stood like a beacon of faith. Farther on was another tiny store, so close to the pavement that it was almost on the road. Then there was a small stone church on the left with a trim cemetery back of it. A sign told us it was Shady Grove Baptist Church.

Soon we entered Hayesville. The road passed around the town square, which had a stately old red brick courthouse in its center. Then it led down a hill and across to the lookout point on the south side of the river, above the construction site of the dam. There a platform had been erected so that people could watch the activity below. A stand with a map showed the future lake's shoreline. Herman and I looked at it intently, figuring the places where water would obliterate the roads, and which of the high hills around it would have a good view of the lake.

Land on both sides of the river had been cleared. Houses and barns were being moved or torn down. Trees were cut, stumps piled and burned. Off to our left the cofferdam would divert the river while the dam was under construction. In addition to the map, the board at the observation post held a drawing under glass. It showed a picture of a slightly curved concrete crescent that would hold the lake, which would cover these lands and provide flood control, electricity, and recreation.

About half the families who had lived in this area had already moved. Whole houses that were small enough to put on rollers and drag to higher ground had already been relocated. Some folks had moved to Franklin or Murphy or to Hiwassee or Blairsville, Georgia. Other people were buying land in Clay County, sometimes to farm on a small place or to live near relatives and look for work. Buildings too large to move easily were torn down. The lumber was carefully stacked with nails drawn, windows and doors laid aside, and roofs saved to be replaced on location. This was at the end of the Depression Era, and all usable materials were recycled. Careful husbandry of resources proved to be helpful as people began to feel shortages occasioned by the war preparations.

Even on Saturday afternoon, the activity was feverish. The trucks and people down below looked small. The barns and houses still standing were toylike in appearance. The fences stood like silent observers of the land that was being stolen from between them. Roads zigzagged across the country. It had been a busy farming area. I felt sorry for the people who were leaving the homes that had belonged in their families for generations. It was sad to think of the change it would make in their daily lives, but it was exciting to consider the advantages the dams were bringing to this region.

We watched until Helen and Dick became restless and Mabel was ready to go home. Herman took his pipe out of his mouth and, holding it cupped in one hand until it cooled, put it in his back pocket. Still gesturing with his right arm and pointing out to my willing eyes the different roads and farmsteads below us, we reluctantly followed Mabel and the girls back to the car for the joke-filled ride back home. It was a wonderful treat for me to see more of the countryside than Brasstown, but even more welcome was the taste of family life that the Estes shared so generously with me.

A few days later, at supper one night, Louise asked if I'd like to ride up to the dam to load a barn on the school truck. They were going to move it down to the place Hickory and Sue Reece had just bought from Glen and Eunice Holland on the hill across Brasstown Creek from the Folk School. The very thought filled me with curiosity and I asked, "How do they move a barn?" No one laughed at my question, though I often felt awkward and naïve when I didn't know what others took for granted. I noticed that most country people lived by observation and experience, and they rarely questioned others.

Patiently Georg explained, "The barn they chose has been taken apart carefully. The rafters are stacked, and parts of the sides are ready to load, along with the doors, loft floor, and other parts. When they bring it down to the Reeces' place, we'll all go over and help them put it up again."

Several of us went with Monroe and Hick Reece to the clearing by the riverbed that would soon be at the bottom of Lake Chatuge. So much of the hope of the Folk School was tied up in the paradox of keeping the beauty of the environment, the strength of the traditions, and the crafts of the area, while introducing better economic opportunities for all. I was excited to be included and to watch the work, both the moving and, weeks later with the help of neighbors, the barn raising.

Just starting out in married life, Hickory and Sue Reece were delighted to have a "new" barn at a price they could afford. We all expected it to crown the gentle hill forever. Looking back up the Hiwassee River valley from its home in Brasstown, it would maintain a gentle dignity of the past despite changes that might surround it.

Friday Night Games

Photo courtesy of the John C. Campbell Folk School Archives, Brasstown, North Carolina.

". . . I heard the upright piano calling from the Community Room
downstairs. Someone was beating out 'There'll Be a Hot Time
in the Old Town Tonight.'"

ONE FRIDAY NIGHT AFTER SUPPER, I went back up to my room in search of something to do. The workweek was over and it was time for fun, but I wasn't sure what was available that evening. I sat down at the small desk by the window to write a letter, but before a word was off my pen, I heard the upright piano calling from the Community Room downstairs. Someone was beating out "There'll Be a Hot Time in the Old Town Tonight."

With a light knock on my door, Helen Mills, a new girl with long dark hair and big brown eyes, looked in. "It's time for Friday Night Games. Do you want to go down with me?" Happy to have company, I glanced in the mirror, smoothed my hair, and joined her. The music had taken a foot-tapping turn. We followed the sound as if it flowed from the Pied Piper's flute, tripping our way down the stairs and into the Community Room.

The floor was cleared. The chairs that customarily stood in rows facing the low dais were now arranged on the platform facing the room. These were hardwood, handturned chairs with the curved back slats and seats woven of white oak splits. On each was inscribed the name of the community individual who had donated the chair in 1927. They stood ready for anyone who might come to watch the games. Other chairs lined the walls of the room, flanking the hot air radiators under the banks of small-paned windows. It was an attractive room. A huge stone fireplace took up much of the far wall, and two large wagon wheels set with electric lights hung from the ceiling.

In 1927 after plans were made to build Keith House as the center for the Folk School, men in Brasstown volunteered to build a community room next to it—a space for community activities, meetings, programs, and social gatherings. Everyone contributed time and materials for construction and worked together on the project. People had given the handmade, straight chairs to furnish the room. The dedication of the Community Room in 1927 had been an occasion for celebration. Now it also provided space for Friday Night Games. Everyone from Brasstown and the surrounding area was welcome. This was their room. It was always open to those who just came to watch, as well as to those who wanted to learn to dance. Many young people from the community came regularly. Some attended the school as day students, others had come from different parts of the mountains and had married at the Folk School and settled in Brasstown to farm or find jobs in the community.

Helen and I sat on the cold radiators with Annie Laurie and Peavine, who had beat us down from their third-story room. Young and old from the community were converging on the activities as evening chores were finished, and there was time for socializing in the last of the long evenings of daylight. The Folk School family gathered, coming from other rooms in Keith House and from homes on the grounds. Most of the girls and women wore bright cotton blouses and full print skirts. Men wore stiffly starched white shirts and blue jeans ironed to a cutting crease.

The faithful school secretary and musician, Harriet Cornwell, was trying out the upright piano next to the fireplace with a series of popular songs that included "Red Sails in the Sunset," one of my favorites. It brought back the music from my boarding-school years and the picture over my roommate's bed. Harriet was always friendly with the students. Now as we chatted on the radiator, she stopped playing and came around to greet us just as Georg and Marguerite entered. "They'll lead the dancing," one of the girls whispered to me.

Harriet turned quickly and went back to the piano. Marguerite went over and gave Harriet the list of dances for the evening. Then Marguerite in her pretty peasant costume circled the floor shooing several groups of young people, who were chattering in congenial groups, off to the sides of the big room. There they stood, expectantly waiting for the dance to begin.

Georg stood with one foot on the raised edge of the platform and watched his wife quietly as he joked with one of the older men who had come to observe the dancing. As soon as Harriet struck up a dance tune, Georg came over to the radiator near the door and asked me to dance.

"I don't know it," I protested shyly.

"I'm going to teach," he said, stretching out his broad, callused palm invitingly. Standing, I put my hand in his, feeling the comfort of his leadership. I was curious and happy to be included, and his Danish friendliness and spontaneous good humor were infectious. I followed him willingly to the center of the Community Room as other couples flocked onto the floor.

The first dance was a "long ways." We lined up in two rows, facing each other. As the music began, the dancers each acknowledged their partners with a slight bow. Georg called out the sequence of moves: swing your partner, arm in arm; pass your partner back to back (do-si-do); take hands and slide, slide, slide between the rows and back to the top; then turn out and skip to the bottom of the line. In my early teen years, I loved the dances like the Virginia Reel, which we sometimes did at parties. The "long ways" were similar and gave me a similar, carefree sense of abandonment. I was breathless and happy as Georg escorted me back to my cooling seat on the radiator.

More dances followed. Everyone participated. If there was a shortage of men and boys, girls paired up. Facing partners in lines of three or six, or in squares of four couples, dancers walked through the steps of each dance as Georg taught it. "Little Man in a Fix" and "Totur" were both lively dances, involving some wild swinging of partners. That first evening I watched as Georg demonstrated them with gusto, ignoring his wife's admonitions to maintain some restraint. Harriet continued to pound out the tunes on the piano, in joyful measures. The dancers stepped and swung until they were forced to a sweaty stop to cool off.

At midevening intermission, everyone rushed to the water fountain or went outside to the terrace by the front door. I went to sit with Louise on the platform, where she had been talking with Lillian Caldwell. Lillian was getting up to go home for the evening, taking her youngest child home for bed. Louise turned to me and began explaining the way in which the Friday Night Games tradition began.

"When Georg Bidstrup arrived at the Folk School in 1926 to direct the farming operation, the school was in its infancy. He was a gymnastics teacher as well as a farmer, and he was recommended to Mrs. Campbell and Marguerite when they visited his brother's folk school in Denmark. Soon after he arrived at the school, Georg told them that in Denmark he found it easier for farm students to enjoy recreation by training them first in gymnastics. So when he wasn't busy with farm work, he began teaching the students simple gymnastics and group exercises in a field in front of Farm House."

The music started again, and both Louise and I left the stage, ready for the next dance. She shepherded me through the next one, which wasn't too difficult, and then left me to ask one of the new girls to dance with her. I looked around, hoping for a partner. Monroe, two of the boy students, and the Stalcup twins from Martin's Creek were coming in the door from outside. I knew they would dance, but I felt too shy to ask any of them. "They probably have girl friends or at least favorite partners," I thought.

Harriet continued to be busy at the piano, and her husband, Gwen, was free. I had talked with him when Louise and I visited at the house he and Harriet were building in Brasstown. He seemed older, and I felt as though I knew him, so I asked if he would do the next dance with me. It proved to be a good choice. Gwen was tall and skillful and willing to teach me the steps he had learned as a student at the Folk School before launching out on his own. His gentleness impressed me and gave me the courage to ask one of the younger girls to dance with me when the music began again.

As Georg taught other dances, I recognized the pleasure most of the students took in learning Scandinavian folk dances and traditional English country-dances. That first evening I watched the more sophisticated dancers, a real cross-section of people: old and young, rich and poor, students and staff, from the Folk School and the community, men and boys, women and girls, friends and strangers.

Fred Smith was another considerate partner. He and his wife, Ruth, had been Folk School students who married and settled in the Brasstown community. They were both artistic and had made many of the furnishings for their home before immersing themselves in the art of raising two charmingly bright little girls. Fred loved to come on Friday nights, but Ruth stayed home with the little ones. Fred helped me with the timing and rhythm of the dances by quietly counting, "one, two, three," for the waltzes, and appropriately for the other dances. For a young person from a sheltered suburban background, it was exhilarating to witness such a cosmopolitan mixture in this country so far away from the home in which I grew up.

The boys at the school were good dancers, especially the twins, Clyde and Claude Stalcup, but my favorite partner was Monroe. He was an excellent dancer and much in demand. As subsequent weeks passed, I found that a variety of partners gave me a real opportunity to know people with whom I would never have become acquainted in any other way. It was standard practice to change partners often. If dancers became too settled in a special group or danced too often with the same partner, Georg would call cheerfully for a "mixer."

That first evening's Friday Night Games came to a close all too soon. Georg called for a "beeg circle." Finally, Monroe came over and asked me to dance. "Come on for the Wagon Wheel," he urged. "I'll show you." He reached out his hand and pulled me to my feet, giving me his comfortable sense of camaraderie. The dance included everyone in a large circle, with the figures danced by couples facing each other in sequence. Then, separating, men and women alternately circled in opposite directions, forming a chain by shaking hands as we met each member of the other circle. This was to the lustily sung tune of "Merrily We Roll Along." It was fun to experience all these different people one at a time and to return each time to Monroe's firm hand, clowning face, and laughing smile. Finally, standing in a circle, holding hands, we sang quietly, "Good Night to You All." Monroe gave my hand a playful good-night shake.

After this first experience with Friday Night Games, I managed to sit at Marguerite's table at dinner, so I could ask her a bit about her experiences in Kentucky before she had joined Mrs. Campbell in establishing a folk school. Marguerite loved to tell a story and launched into her account gladly.

"After I graduated from college, I wanted to do something helpful for the Appalachian people in eastern Kentucky. I grew up in Cincinnati, so I knew that there were a number of private schools in small settlements in the mountains. Philanthropists established them around the turn of the century to provide education and health care for the mountain people. I had always enjoyed horseback riding and was interested in the Frontier Nursing Service based at the Pine Mountain Settlement School, so I volunteered for a job there."

I noted our different ways of choosing work after college. Perhaps it was living through the Depression years or my decision to shelve books in the library instead of asking my parents for spending money that gave me a sense of identity with working people. Marguerite, on the other hand, had the privileged sense of noblesse oblige.

She continued, "It was rough terrain, not as beautiful or as open as this country. The mountains are steeper, the land more difficult to farm. I had to travel on my horse up narrow trails and along small creek beds. I was not a nurse, but I visited families to help teach hygiene, better homemaking, and childcare. Many isolated communities formed on the edge of coal-mining country. The people had quaint expressions, and I made every effort to jot many of them in my notebook. I wrote short descriptions of the people so I would remember them each time I visited."

She paused, gave her attention to others at the table, and then continued in her precise fashion. "I loved the people and made many friends. One of my favorites was Aunt Sal. She was over sixty years old and lived alone in a very small log house perched on the side of a steep mountain. A huge, smooth gray rock spread out along the house, and beside it was a clear mountain stream. Aunt Sal had found the spring there that supplied her with drinking and cooking water. Below the spring, she did her laundry and spread the clothes on the rock surface to dry in the sun. She raised a family up there, but her husband died, and her daughter married and moved further down the mountain. So, she lived alone, a courageous lady. I really loved to visit her. Aunt Sal taught me so much about rural life."

The story had gone on through most of the dinner hour, but I was curious to know more. I trailed Marguerite back to her office saying, "I hate to take up more of your time, Marguerite, but I'd really like to know why you call the dances on Friday night 'games.'"

She sat down behind her desk in the small office she shared with Mrs. Campbell and continued her story: "In Kentucky there was so little money and so little opportunity to make a living that many farmers began manufacturing whiskey from their home-grown corn. It was illegal, but they needed the income and there was a ready market. Often they were caught and sent to prison. Law-abiding people in the community developed ways of avoiding any appearance of contact with the moonshiners, boot-leggers, and drinkers. At the Pine Mountain school, they avoided criticism from the church-goers by playing 'play-party games' instead of dancing, because at dances there was always some drinking to accompany the fun.

"After Mrs. Campbell asked me to accompany her to the Scandinavian countries to study the rural folk schools, we discovered how dancing plays an important part in preserving the culture of a country. We decided that we would teach folk dancing here at the Folk School, and to avoid any confusion with activities that often accompany drinking, we decided to call our recreation 'games' instead of 'dances.'"

After the students became comfortable with gymnastics, Marguerite joined the teaching of games. They added simple singing games such as London Bridge and Drop the Handkerchief. Later they taught sedate English country contras, or "long ways," and Danish country-dances. Marguerite and Mrs. Campbell visited Cecil Sharp in England in 1923, following their visit to Scandinavian folk schools. Cecil Sharp and Olive Campbell had collaborated in collecting ballads in Appalachia when the Campbells were working in the mountains before World War I. At Sharp's summer school in the south of England, they learned the complexities of English folk dancing.

Gradually Georg Bidstrup and Marguerite Butler formed a recreation team. They were married at the Folk School in 1936. They made an interesting couple at the weekly dances. Georg was an expert at involving participation, while Marguerite was the perfectionist, who kept everyone in line. A patient careful teacher, she gave clear and exacting directions and waited until every dancer was in the correct position and attitude before she would proceed. When they included an occasional American square dance, she allowed no clogging. To avoid resemblance to rowdy square dancing, they taught the graceful sliding step.

Marguerite was very critical of the square dancing led by Bascom Lunsford, which was beginning to gain popularity in and around Asheville. She thought it lacked dignity.

Often, if the dance was not proceeding as Marguerite thought it should, she clapped her hands and held up the music, so the dancers could regroup and try again. She had been a perfectionistic super-achiever all her life, and the trait certainly surfaced in her dances. Always she kept in mind the high standards she and Mrs. Campbell had observed at Cecil Sharp's school in England.

"Dargasson" was an English country-dance for eight. The music was captivating, urging participation by all. Each dancer was clearly visible, spread out in a single file, with each line of four facing each other diagonally. Because everyone aspired to do the dance, there was always a race for a place in line. Although occasionally I managed to get in the right position first, my performance rarely met Marguerite's standards. Many times she stopped the music, asked me to sit down, and called for a better dancer to take my place. Although she did the same with other dancers, I felt deeply humiliated, disappointed, and somewhat rejected by Marguerite.

Thanks to Georg and Marguerite Bidstrup, recreation and dance became important parts of many students' lives. They were essential to the balanced country living that the Folk School was designed to teach. In my enthusiasm after one enjoyable evening, I asked Monroe, who had certainly become my favorite partner, "Don't you just love Friday nights, Muns? The dancing is such fun!"

He hesitated. "I don't know. I think it's pretty silly. I really liked it better down at Hiwassee Dam. There they did square dancing for the people who came from away to build the dam. A group of us boys had a jug band and went down there last year to make music for the dances. I think that was really fun. At home though, we didn't have time for this foolishness. Work was what was important." I was surprised by his answer and always disappointed when he chose to skip a Friday night of games. The evening came to be an exclamation point in each week for me as I became more and more a part of the school family and the community.

Life in Keith House

"In the winter of 1925, Mrs. Campbell and Marguerite Butler . . . held community meetings and classes in the tiny living room. People . . . came in hopes that they would learn how to live richer lives."

ADJOINING THE COMMUNITY ROOM, where we danced Friday Night Games, was Keith House, the center of Folk School life. It had an interesting history. When the location of the Folk School was chosen in the beautiful autumn months of 1924, the only habitable building on the land was Farm House. In the winter of 1925, Mrs. Campbell and Marguerite Butler established a home there and held community meetings and classes in the tiny living room. People walked for miles to learn about the school. They crowded in and sat wherever they could perch, much like hungry birds. They came for classes about better farming and opportunities for extra income. They came in hopes that they would learn how to live richer lives. Soon it became evident that Farm House was not large enough for all the neighbors who came from near and far to the programs and meetings. Plans were made and money sought for a building to provide classrooms, administrative space, and a girls' dormitory. Keith House was built in 1927 with money from generous Yankee friends, and it was named in honor of the donors. Then the Community Room was built next to Keith House by neighbors who were generous with their time and materials.

Although Keith House was the center of Folk School life, at night most of the staff went home to a variety of small houses scattered across the approximately 360 acres of farmland and woods. The buildings all belonged to the school, but each showed the individuality of the couple or family living there. In the large four-story tan clapboard building that was Keith House, there were classrooms, bedrooms, a kitchen and dining room, offices, a sales room, weaving rooms, a living room, and other gathering places. The architecture of the building was appropriate for the country, but not typical of any region. A fieldstone foundation and a flat, rock terrace at the entrance gave the building a local flavor. The Community Room stood at one side of the entrance. On the other side and half below ground level were the kitchen, pantry, dining room, lavatories, furnace, storeroom, and laundry.

Keith House also functioned as the girls' dormitory. There were three or four cots in each of the large rooms on the second floor and several in each of the rooms under the eaves on the third floor. A common bathroom and shower was on the attic floor. Only elderly Miss Gaines at one end of the hall and I at the other had our own semiprivate bathroom on the second floor. The privilege of privacy and our New England roots set us apart from the girl students and gave us common ground as staff members.

The girls counted on Miss Gaines for comfort and direction, but they welcomed me to their rooms with little or no fanfare. One night I had a special invitation to play Rook and listen to jokes in one of the bedrooms at the top of the house. I had never much cared for dirty jokes or shady stories, but I really wanted to be included so I accepted the invitation.

The ringleader was a bright energetic farm girl from the South Carolina edge of the mountains. Annie Laurie was the only girl in a family of brothers and was an unabashed teller of tales. She was a bit of a tomboy with short, straight blond hair and a particularly raw earthy humor distilled from farm life. Her slang terms for bodily functions and sexual references passed embarrassingly over my head. Even to this day I couldn't possibly tell you the meaning of most of her words or the gist of the jokes. Not only did my sheltered background embarrass me, but also I had no idea what she was talking about most of the time. I enjoyed the companionship though, and laughed as appropriately as I was able.

The girls explained that these jokes were nothing compared to the ones the boys could tell. Several girls insisted that Monroe was adept at barnyard and bathroom humor, and that he was the best at pulling practical jokes on others. When I protested that I had never heard that side of his conversation, they agreed that he probably held his tongue in check when I was around.

One evening Annie Laurie, my jokester friend, told me that Monroe and Gene, one of the students in the boys' dorm at Mill House, had asked her if she'd slip out and play Rook some night in Monroe's room at Tower House. She said she had told Gene that we wanted to play cards and didn't really know many games, so he had invited her to bring me and come down after everyone else was in bed. She begged me to go with her. It sounded like fun and was a dare of sorts so I agreed.

Keith House was dark and quiet at nine or ten o'clock. We slipped out of a dormitory window and down the fire escape ladder to the ground at the entrance to the house. Silently, suppressing giggles, we walked through the woods to the barns and Tower House, which held a dorm room over the Blacksmith Shop. It was very quiet and dark, and it never occurred to us that we might be discovered. Lights were out, and everyone else was safely in bed and asleep.

In response to our soft knock, Monroe called, "Come in. Welcome to my humble abode." We made our way up the narrow stairway to his large room. There were dark bare windows on all four sides and a huge stone fireplace. The rich odor of a blazing fire filled the room. Monroe and Gene were roasting wieners and toasting marshmallows. In their most gentlemanly fashion, they offered us each a toasting fork and kibitzed as we cooked the food to our individual tastes. We washed down the hot dogs with strong coffee from a blue enamel pot sitting on the hearth, and we finished the feast with toasted marshmallows, burned to a crisp on the outside but sticky and sweet inside.

Finally, we played Rook for a while. We girls lost in spite of our best efforts. We all laughed a lot. Then, afraid we might be missed back at the dormitory if we stayed too long, we said good night and made our way back along the narrow path through the dark silent woods. A barn owl hooted as we passed and, guilt-filled as I felt, it startled me. The nighttime lark was definitely the most adventurous experience I ever had in a school setting and was totally out of character for me, but it made me one of the girls. My companion in crime just laughed and joked when I confessed my feelings, and she retorted, "We didn't hurt anyone, did we?"

At other times, I was a responsible member of the staff. The family atmosphere of the school dimmed the line between students and faculty, but differences in responsibilities were well defined. Two or three girls worked with me in the shop sometimes, finishing the carvings and helping in other ways as needed. Usually after lunch, we took a short break before going back to work, but one day I had so much to do that I went back before anyone else had returned.

I was quietly assembling a rush order for carvings that needed to go out in the afternoon mail when I heard the two girls who were assigned to the shop sit down on the back steps in the autumn sunshine to rest before coming in to work. Before I could make my presence known, they began talking confidentially. I felt trapped, unwilling to reveal myself for fear of embarrassing them, but glad to give them a chance to talk to each other confidentially.

Eulene's voice was low and gentle. "Don't you hate it when they talk about us at lunch as if we aren't really there?" she asked.

"What do you mean?" came Anna Jean's more strident and high-pitched reply.

"Well, all the staff want to get some of us to do their work, and that's all right because we are working for our room and board and schooling. But Mrs. Campbell and Marguerite talk back and forth from table to table about which of us girls they want to work where. Sometimes they even argue as if they want to get the best, and I feel strange, like I'm being traded back and forth," Eulene replied calmly.

"I don't pay it no mind. There really isn't any harm intended. They're just joking and comparing jobs that need to be done. Who are you going to do for in the morning?" Anna Jean was oblivious to any embarrassment about the exchange between the ladies at meals.

"Mrs. Campbell spoke for me. She needs some housecleaning done and she likes for me to help because I'm tall and can reach those high places that she has to use a step stool to get to. I just love all the pretty things at Farm House anyway. Who are you assigned to?" Eulene was proud to be chosen for her height and by Mrs. Campbell.

Competitively, Anna Jean came back quickly, "Marguerite. She likes me 'cause I'm so fast. We have to change all the beds in the boys' dormitory and bring them up to the laundry. I don't mind. I like to feel that I'm really doing something, and you never can tell what you'll find in the boys' rooms. Last time I helped her clean, we found an old beer can, and you should have seen her face. But I like Marguerite. She's real good when I have the headache and lets me take off early when it's that time."

"She is more understanding with the girls, it seems, but I like to hear Mrs. Campbell talk. She always has some interesting story to tell about faraway places or ideas. I think that's why she likes teaching the boys. She enjoys discussing business and politics with them."

"Did you know that before her husband got sick they had two little daughters, who died when they were babies? I think that's why she takes to the students. They are the children she lost." Eulene was thoughtful.

"I didn't know that. I don't think Marguerite and Georg will have any children, do you? She's really too old, and that's too bad. He likes the little ones who come with the carvers on Thursday and those who come to watch the games."

"Well, I'm glad to be working at Farm House this week. The other day Mrs. Campbell was fixing up the living room. She had me to hang a beautiful woven blanket in that space over the fireplace, and then she put a pottery bowl of fall leaf branches right on one side. She said it was an arrangement like they do overseas somewhere, but it was pretty. I'd never have thought to do anything like that."

"Marguerite has a lot of good ideas about housekeeping, too. We're going to make scrapbooks of how we want to fix our own homes sometime, if I'm lucky enough to catch someone and ever make a place for myself." Anna Jean laughed hoarsely.

The comparisons took a turn toward amused tolerance, and Eulene added, "Sometimes we move that orange Jugtown pottery on the dining room sideboard just a little bit to see what she will do. Sure enough, the first time Marguerite passes she notices the jugs out of place and puts them back just exactly right."

"I helped Marguerite cook Sunday breakfast for company, down at Mill House last week. I fried the bacon, and do you know, she wants it fried up with every single piece straight as a board and perfectly crisp. Mrs. Campbell just laughed and said she liked hers done up curly and twisted. She and Marguerite certainly are a pair, different as day and night."

"They both care about the way things look though. The boys have their ways to aggravate Marguerite, too. They throw down their little bitty pieces of gum paper, and she never misses picking up each little scrap."

"Did you see her the day Ralph and Loyal rode their horses over to Keith House?"

"Yes, I did. She was mad as a hornet and told them to go back home and not ride around the school any more. It was a sight. She is very particular about appearances and didn't want the horses messing up the drive in front of Keith House. Sometimes I wonder how much she welcomes the Brasstown young people who are not students here."

"Right you are, Eulene, old girl. I wonder too, but let's get to work now. We've jawed long enough," Anna Jean concluded, and they came in.

They didn't express any surprise at finding me already at work, and I appreciated the opportunity to overhear their thoughtful exchange of opinions. They were similar to others I had already heard in one form or another, so we just didn't say anything about the conversation.

Louise expressed some surprise at my congeniality with the students. She had expected Mr. Deschamps's daughter, Carol, who had just graduated from Berea College, to be back at home so that I would have a companion with whom I could share intellectual interests, but Carol surprised everyone with a wedding at Rock House early that autumn. So, I found companionship with students. Despite our diverse backgrounds, I appreciated the friendly acceptance I felt and the opportunity to know young people close to my own age whose life experiences had been so different from my own.

Many of them had skills I had never learned. Sewing was one of them. At the end of October, a Halloween party was planned in addition to the regular Friday Night Games. Some would wear costumes, and all the girls were making their own long dresses from flowered feed sacks. When I bemoaned the fact that I didn't know how to make a dress, Mabel Scroggs, who was a younger day student living at home in Brasstown, volunteered to help me. I managed to get the sacks, wash, and iron them. Mabel brought a pattern and helped me cut out my dress, and then she took it home to sew the seams on the machine, bringing it back for me to hem in time for the party. We all had a great time, although to my dismay, Monroe was not there. Later he confessed to me quietly that he had found other ways to celebrate Halloween in the usual mischievous style of the country.

Miss Gaines also helped me to become part of my new world. She combined her talents as stern taskmaster and warm comforter. Her small room at the end of the hall on the second floor of Keith House was a refuge for the girls when they needed it. They could go in and talk over their problems or tell her their troubles in utmost confidence. She listened without making judgments or giving advice.

Strictly off limits at other times to anyone else, it was the haven to which Miss Gaines retired when her work was done. There she curled up with a book and her big black and white cat, Scampo. Serene, confident, and cheerful, with a peaceful common sense about life, Miss Gaines had two very important roles at the school. She had been recruited by Marguerite from the Pratt Institute in Brooklyn, New York, and was well qualified as a dietician and teacher. She inspired the girls to cook imaginative and thrifty, nutritious meals with whatever the farm produced. She was a stern taskmaster in that capacity, but as housemother, she was warmly nurturing.

Resourceful New Englander that she was, she discovered that I had my driver's license and could drive the Folk School car. She put in a bid for my services and borrowed me for an afternoon to do the necessary marketing in Murphy. As we traveled, I found that she didn't miss anything and kept me well informed by pointing out the sights and her opinions of them.

"This road, following the Hiwassee River down to Murphy, is perhaps one of the most beautiful drives I have ever had the fun of using on a regular basis," she would coo almost every week. "It makes doing the marketing a real pleasure."

There was no supermarket, although a small A&P had recently edged into a tiny space between run-down shops. There they sold beer by the case for the benefit of construction workers who had moved into the area to build the TVA dams. It never mattered to her that I had just received my driver's license. "Just pull in there in front of the A&P," she ordered. The space was narrow. With fear and trembling, I edged in between a pickup truck and an old Ford, wondering if I would ever be able to back out into the street.

She vowed that the A&P had the best and cheapest meat in town, but after looking over the meat counter, she bought a few staples and said she was ready to go to Hembree's Meat Market on Valley River Avenue. "It wasn't fresh at the A&P today," she explained.

There was a visit to Mattox's Hardware for some hooks and a flashlight and to Mauney's Drugstore for aspirin and cough syrup. Each stop meant more practice in backing and parking. If a spot was accessible to the most experienced driver in the world, she was sure it was possible for me; I had to put the car there. She wouldn't take no for an answer. I became most appreciative of the driving expertise Miss Gaines taught me, even though she had never driven herself.

From that day on, each week we shopped thriftily for things the school did not provide for itself. Miss Gaines knew where to find the best buys for everything on her list. With her basket on her arm and a frugal eye for bargains, she gathered the necessary supplies with patience. Then we did the weekly errands for all the Folk School family.

Miss Gaines did not impose on me the protective authority she reserved for "her girls" at Keith House. She treated me more as a colleague on the staff, albeit one in need of her guidance. However, she always refused to include me in her cooking classes as if that were beneath me. We shared a love of plants, and sometimes she told me about the flowers she tended in boxes around the edge of her sunken kitchen porch. When frost threatened, she potted the red geraniums and kept them on a sunny shelf in her room.

During my stay at Keith House, we developed a camaraderie that belied the years that separated us. Perhaps our Yankee background made for an understanding of gruff communication and provided us both with a way of evaluating people and liking them for their differences.

In a number of cases, it was Miss Gaines who gave me a perspective on other relationships. She was fiercely loyal to Marguerite and not bothered, as I was, by her critical personality. She was motherly toward Georg, as well as toward all the students. She was particularly fond of Monroe and protective toward him because he had come to the school as a small sixteen year old. Five years in this nourishing environment had turned him from a bright high school valedictorian into a responsible man on whom she could rely for all the special farm products she needed in the kitchen. Toward Mrs. Campbell, she exhibited amused tolerance for dietary whims. Her respect for the director's intellectual approach to life was mellowed by her concern for Mrs. Campbell's health. In any case, Miss Gaines won my respect. Our friendship lasted many years after I left the school.

I enjoyed living in Keith House. My little room was comfortable and convenient, and I liked being in the middle of everything that was going on and being near friends close to my own age. Also, I valued my time with Miss Gaines and appreciated her talent for keeping everyone's feet on the ground. I felt completely at home in Keith House, so I was surprised one day by an invitation to move.

Farm House

"It really stains. . . . Black walnut is the vegetable dye we use to get shades of tan and brown for weaving. . . . Louise scoured the fields and woods for herbs and glasses that would yield natural dyes."

THE AIR WAS CLEAR AND BRIGHT; the sky, a deep October blue; and the clouds, as white as innocence. Late one afternoon in the latter part of the month, Gayle Isensee joined the Folk School staff. Plainly dressed, long-faced and breathless, Gayle blew in just in time for supper. She was a semiretired nurse from western Pennsylvania, who was eager to initiate an educational health and nursing service for the community and surrounding countryside. Gifted with words, a facile mouth, and earnest brown eyes, Gayle regaled us with tales of her trip from Pennsylvania. "You wouldn't believe how long it took me to drive from Asheville. I thought I had already arrived when I reached the North Carolina line up there below Bristol, Tennessee. I spent last night in Virginia with an old friend from nursing school. I really didn't think I had so much further to go, but I was mistaken. It's a long way from Asheville, especially when you get to the Nantahala Gorge. That's one twisty road." She drew a long breath.

That night Gayle stayed at Farm House with Mrs. Campbell and Louise. They had planned for her to live there, so that Mrs. Campbell would not be alone when Louise made her annual trip up north for two months during the winter. Gayle was a competent nurse and a friendly woman who never met a stranger. As Louise helped her unpack in the guest room that evening, Gayle confided her hopes and fears. Back in Pennsylvania, she had left an elderly widower father on whom she kept a watchful eye. She expected him to join her here eventually.

Louise took me aside quietly the next morning. "Would you mind giving up your room in Keith House to Gayle? Mrs. Campbell wants you to come and live with us at Farm House. Gayle needs to be close to a telephone, so that she can be reached if someone in the community gets sick in the night, and so that she can monitor her father's well-being back home."

Later I wondered about this explanation of Gayle's need for a telephone. Telephones were scarce in the country. Usually people drove to the house of a doctor or nurse in search of help in an emergency. However, although Gayle's need to be available for a long-distance call seemed valid, I suspected that Mrs. Campbell feared the nurse's constant chatter might become tiresome, but she wouldn't have thought of hurting Gayle's feelings. However, I was pleased to be invited to join Louise and Mrs. Campbell at Farm House for whatever reason. We would make an interesting trio, twenty years separating each of us in age, although our Yankee educations united us in background. Louise assured me that in the years she had lived with Mrs. Campbell, she had gathered more wisdom than she had in all her four years of college at Columbia University. Living in the Farm House also validated my status as a staff member rather than as a student at the Folk School. As the middle child in my birth family, I always seemed to steer a path of compromise between divergent groups. That year I went back and forth between the students of my own age group and the staff of various ages and backgrounds.

Farm House was typical of mountain houses with a basic two-story structure and an ell addition built at the back. It appeared that before the addition there had been two main rooms downstairs and two bedrooms upstairs, with a stone chimney and fireplaces in the center of the house. In 1941, it had a white clapboard exterior and a long front porch. Mrs. Campbell used the newer addition at the back of the house for most of her daily living activities. She ate breakfast, tea, and most suppers there in the long dining room that separated the kitchen from the rest of the house. However, she welcomed students to all parts of her house. In many ways it was a demonstration of what a mountain home could be, combining artistry, simplicity, and practicality.

The next afternoon I gathered my possessions and bade a regretful farewell to my haven at Keith House. After making my daily trip to the post office, I circled the driveway at Farm House. I intended to deposit my suitcase and miscellaneous collection of jackets and papers on the front porch before returning the car to the garage behind Farm House. As I passed the ramshackle shed that had been converted into a garage, I noticed that a scarlet trumpet vine threatened to engulf one whole side. There Mrs. Campbell, completely covered by a bright gingham apron and equipped with huge pruning shears, was valiantly trying to trim the vine back into submission. I stopped the car and jumped out.

"May I help?" She handed me the pruning hook graciously and stepped back to direct my work. Soon we had the invader under temporary control.

It was a good beginning. They made me one of their family at once, giving me a little room at the back of the house over the kitchen. It was accessible either through the bathroom we all three shared, or by way of the backstairs to the sleeping porch. With two ways out and two windows over my bed, I didn't even think of the big rope that had afforded emergency escape from my little room in Keith House. Louise and Mrs. Campbell each had a large bedroom at the top of the narrow stairway from the living room. Their windows opened over the front porch, but both women preferred to sleep in the open air. They deserted their warm beds and their comfortable front rooms for the sleeping porch almost year round. They invited me to take the little half bed at the top of the back stairs onto the porch, but I valued my privacy and preferred my own little room.

Through the high windows over my antique dusty-pink spool bed, I could see the barns and Tower House over the Blacksmith Shop. My room became a refuge for me. It was furnished with a small black walnut desk, a straight chair, an uncomfortable little rocker, and a Franklin Stove that would relinquish some heat if I chose to stay in my room long enough to warrant the trouble of building a fire.

Farm House became dear to me. Mrs. Campbell had a wonderful gift of cheerfulness. Her good spirits were infectious, never intrusive. She confronted every household crisis with gallant ingenuity. The antique coal furnace, in the dug-out basement under the original house, chugged and heaved and occasionally wheezed into a temporary collapse. With a working fireplace in each room, we could press any one of them into service, as the occasion demanded. Building a wood fire required some skill and the ability to improvise, but both Louise and Mrs. Campbell were experienced, and I soon acquired the knack.

We used the dining room in the middle of the house most consistently. When the furnace was healthy, even if there was no fire roaring in the fireplace, it was the warmest room. For cheer and light cooking we used the fireplace there regularly. Smooth white cement covered the original rock construction of the chimney and in place of a mantel, the Danish motto *Har du reist og tretet dig, kom sid ned og hvil hos mig* was neatly lettered in black. Mrs. Campbell gladly translated: "After you travel and become tired, come sit down and rest with me."

Often in the morning when I came down for breakfast, I found the Chinese copper teapot purring on the hearth. A crude wrought iron toaster, laden with two pieces of homemade oatmeal bread from Miss Gaines' kitchen, swiveled in front of the flames. Sometimes we added soft-boiled eggs in the shell, resting in eggcups of Danish porcelain, or maybe applesauce in the morning-glory cups from Japan. Breakfast was always elegant but modest, and never routine.

As the junior member of the team, I always washed the dishes and straightened up after the morning meal. Then we each went our separate ways for the day's routine, first to Morning Song and then to work as it unfolded. The noon meal was at Keith House. In the afternoons after I finished at the shop, I fed the chickens and gathered the eggs in the chicken houses above Farm House. Then I'd swing over the fence, cross the pasture, and come down into the backyard of Farm House.

One afternoon just before Thanksgiving, I found Mrs. Campbell and Louise working beneath a fledgling black walnut tree in the yard outside the kitchen door. There was a bushel basket on the ground, and they were tossing the black walnuts into it. The previous week the ground had been covered with green-hulled walnuts. Now they had ripened; the hulls were soft, black, and soggy.

"Look at this wealth!" Mrs. Campbell's voice rang with pleasure. "This is the first year it has borne nuts, and they are plentiful. Put on some gloves and help if you'd like. The gloves are on the table on the back porch."

I followed her suggestion, but soon tired of the gloves and dropped them on the ground. The hulls of the nuts that had fallen from the tree were a rich dark brown and were soft and squishy. We were tossing them into a bushel basket. After a few tosses, I saw that my hands were stained a dark mahogany.

"You'd better try to get that juice off before it dries," Louise warned. "It really stains. You'll have a hard time getting your hands clean. Black walnut is the vegetable dye we use to get shades of tan and brown for weaving."

I was amazed at how the nuts made my hands chocolate colored, but I was even more surprised at the rich harvest from that tree. We spread all the walnuts out on the floor of the loft above the garage. When they dried a bit, I brought them in, bucket by bucket, after breaking off the dried hulls. At night Mrs. Campbell would hunker down on the hearth and crack them with a hammer. She could split the hard shell neatly and pick out large pieces of nutmeat. When I tried to do the same, I was apt to smash the meat into tiny crumbs, so usually Louise and I deferred to the master nutcracker.

Afternoons brought different glimpses of my housemates. Louise scoured the fields and woods for herbs and grasses that would yield natural dyes. I was amazed to find that the ripe broom sedge that covered many worn-out fields yielded a bright yellow dye when boiled in a huge iron pot. Louise tied her harvest in bunches that she hung to dry from the rafters on the small screened back porch. Other times she planned a simple supper for a visiting friend and bustled efficiently in the kitchen, concocting a casserole and a salad.

At the table in the dining room, Mrs. Campbell caught up on personal correspondence, her small script filling each page with lines almost touching each other. Usually when I appeared for tea, she stopped and swept the unfinished letter and writing materials into a graceful open basket with a swooping handle that she placed beside her chair. She pulled the tray holding cups, tea, sugar, cream, and small biscuits toward her, and taking the purring teapot from the hearth, prepared to pour. "I thought we'd have Chinese tea this afternoon. Would you prefer smoky or jasmine?"

Louise usually joined us. We each had a favorite fine china cup and our own cloth napkin in its carved ring. The sterling silver teaspoons were of the same vintage as those of my grandmother. I had used them as a child, so for me a bit of nostalgia accompanied this afternoon ritual. Mrs. Campbell always reserved for herself one special spoon with just the right bowl. She was a connoisseur of fine teas and varied her selection so that after a time I, too, could choose among them. No matter how simple a menu, whether for breakfast, tea, or supper, the way in which it was served brought satisfaction to her New England sense of propriety.

Louise and Mrs. Campbell sometimes preferred to fix their own suppers, but I almost invariably went to Keith House for a substantial meal and the evening activities there. One afternoon I arrived for tea as Mrs. Campbell was sketching a large sitting rabbit.

"The Smithsonian Institution in Washington, D.C., is having a special exhibition for the visually impaired," she said. "They have asked if we can send a piece for the display. I'm sure you have met Jack Hall, who carves the beautiful windblown horses and other animals. I am hoping Jack will carve a sitting rabbit that visitors with limited sight can feel so they can get the sensation of an animal at rest, but tensed to jump. What do you think?"

"I'd love to see what he can do," I hedged. "In your sketch the rabbit certainly looks lifelike and ready to spring, even just on paper. Do you think Jack can carve it to be like that?"

"We'll see," she responded.

A few weeks later at teatime, she was beaming. A large rabbit carved of black walnut wood was on the tea table in front of her.

"Close your eyes and feel it," she commanded.

I ran my hand slowly over the rounded back, feeling the lines and indentations, soft and smooth, with short, fine curvy cuts that felt like fur. The rabbit was about the size of a basketball and rested firmly on its haunches. Running my hand up its rounded back to the cocked head, I felt the tension in the long ears raised to listen. Across the rounded nose and down the chest to the taut muscles in legs poised to jump, I felt the life inherent in the carving.

"It's great," I sighed. "Jack is really good, isn't he?"

"I believe he has much potential. I love his carvings. He seems so able to tackle new things and to put across his feeling of pleasure in his work."

Mrs. Campbell loved to carve also and always had some figure in progress: a Saint Francis, a carving of the Christmas babe and Mary, or some other quite original piece. That winter she carved fruit pieces for a basket centerpiece. For her birthday, I surprised her with a carving of crab apples done by Fred Smith, the former student living in Brasstown who often helped me with the rhythm of the Friday night dances. She had been encouraging him to do flat carvings of apple blossoms on each end of serving trays. For many subsequent years, he carved a living for his family using designs from nature, elaborating and improving on all that he learned at the Folk School.

One sunny afternoon early in December, I arrived breathless and starving for tea, only to find nothing in the offing. Mrs. Campbell called a cheery greeting from the living room, and I went around the stairway to find her standing on a ladder in front of the fireplace. She had hung one of Granny Donalsen's animal blankets from the ceiling molding. The soft tan woven background was appliquéd with fanciful crocheted animals of all colors scattered over it. On the mantel was a long shallow pottery dish in which she had arranged small branches of bright maple leaves over a base of dark green evergreen.

"What do you think?" she asked, tilting her head to one side and cocking one eye in a wise and knowing look that I found quite enchanting.

She waited for my comment, and I knew she really wanted honesty. She valued others' opinions and never seemed offended by constructive criticism.

"It's beautiful," I replied. "It shows how simple things can be arranged artistically. Now would you like a hand in getting down from that ladder?"

She laughed heartily and climbed down. Her ready laugh and forthright comments gave me a sense of perspective in an environment that was still new to me. Her demeanor was encouraging to others as well. One morning we had bread instead of the usual toast, and before we had finished, Oscar Cantrell knocked at the back door and came in, hat in hand.

"I came by to fix that toaster," he explained. "What's the problem with it?" He leaned down to pick it up from the hearth, spinning the brackets with one finger.

"I see. The pin that holds it is bent. I'll make a new one and have it back to you this afternoon. While I'm here, do you want me to look at the garage doors? The hinges you designed are ready, and I need to measure to see how big to make the doors." He passed his hand across his tanned face as if to wipe cobwebs from his eyes. That gesture was as characteristic of him as his wonderful, broad grin.

Oscar was born and raised in Brasstown and began his career as a blacksmith in the community. He continued in that role for the school and was also very creative and ingenious at mending and fixing small machines and repairing parts. Mrs. Campbell relied on him both to weld the small brass and copper pots she had collected in her travels and to design whatever iron hinges and other iron artifacts she needed. With a smile on his weathered face, he liked to say that he was spending more and more time at his forge designing and making ornamental iron pieces than on the farm or as a traditional blacksmith. As farm foreman, blacksmith, and artisan, he taught the boys practical skills with great patience.

Some afternoons, especially when Louise was busy elsewhere, as well as during the two months she spent up north, Mrs. Campbell and I talked. We had very similar values and interests. She believed passionately in education, democracy, conservation, and the cooperative sharing of work and profits in industry, as did I. The changes that were imminent both in the Tennessee Valley and in the country at large made for lively discussions. I was excited about the prospects of economic renewal of the land. She was too, but she still had nostalgia for the quaint ways of the past and particularly for the traces of Elizabethan England in Appalachian music and customs.

The outbreak of war grieved us both, but since Mrs. Campbell had lived through the First World War, she was acutely aware of the drastic changes war would bring to our lives, although I was not. From time to time we philosophized, and I discovered that Louise was right when she told me that Olive Campbell was a veritable encyclopedia of miscellaneous information. Indeed she and I left no subject untouched. Whatever she had on hand, it was always food for thought. Furthermore, she valued opinions and questions. Nothing she offered had to be swallowed whole.

She was interested in my opinions, in my work at college, and in my reasons for coming to Brasstown. One afternoon we talked about the ways in which paid advertising influences the choice of articles in magazines, a subject that had fascinated me in my college study of the contemporary press. I was disappointed that she was less interested in the subtle ways in which values are shaped than in the direct influence of good teaching. She had a wonderful gift of teaching and had wisely chosen the school's motto, "to enrich, enliven, and enlighten."

I was glad Mrs. Campbell had invited me to share Farm House with her. The sense of security I felt there extended into my work in the shop, on the farm, and in the community. The adage over the fireplace, "After you travel and become tired, come sit down and rest with me," was a treasured message. Mrs. Campbell made Farm House home for me.

Pearl Harbor

"I was living with Mrs. Campbell at Farm House, which was on Monroe's way to . . . Tower House."

By December, Monroe and I had become good friends. Every evening as we waited for the supper bell to ring, we shared the *Asheville Citizen* crossword puzzle at the corner table in the Keith House living room. We thoroughly enjoyed this cooperative endeavor, and the rest of the Folk School family considered it our territory and rarely kibitzed. Side by side, we shared an interesting combination of vocabularies. His was practical, nature-oriented, and augmented by a good acquaintance with crossword idiom. I supplied the literary, art, language, and geographical components.

"A shaping tool, three letters?"

"Adz. A fourteen-line rhymed poem?"

"Sonnet."

I was living with Mrs. Campbell at Farm House, which was on Monroe's way to his own bachelor's pad at Tower House. Often after supper and the evening activities, we walked the narrow, winding path through the woods together. He scorned a flashlight, having grown up in the country without one. I soon learned to gauge direction and keep to the path by the feel of the ground. The red leather shoes I had made for myself in the shop were wide and comfortable. The soles were unpadded so that my feet sensed each twisting curve and indentation in the path. We walked easily together, sometimes hand in hand, sometimes arm in arm, but most often freely and independently. It was good to compare experiences and impressions of our different days as we wended our way home.

On Sunday afternoons, it was the custom for all of the Folk School young people to walk together in couples or groups. Hardly anyone our age in the country had a car unless, of course, it was work-essential. One warm afternoon in December after dinner, we started out from Keith House as a group. We made our way down the winding gravel road. We crossed the bridge over Brasstown Creek, and stopped to lean over the rails and throw small sticks and leaves to float under and out the other side. The gentle sound of the running water was peaceful, and the air was damp and fresh.

We lingered a bit for refreshment at Quedor Caldwell's store. Monroe purchased a can of Prince Albert cigarette tobacco and some papers to roll his own. Several girls bought penny candy or five-cent Hershey bars, but I wasn't hungry so soon after Sunday dinner. As we left the store, we parted into two groups. Some turned left to walk down Highway 64 to the bridge over the Hiwassee River and into Cherokee County. The rest of us turned right and walked toward the Mountain Valley Creamery two miles up the highway. There were very few houses along the road after we passed the stores and went around a sharp curve. The Zimmerman house was about a mile along the way, a white weathered house with an open front porch and its barns across the street. No one was stirring on Sunday afternoon.

On this mild December day, a bit overcast, but certainly not cold, I wore the light windbreaker jacket that I lived in most of that winter. We headed upstream to the plant where the locally produced milk was pasteurized and bottled. As we walked, sometimes dawdling a bit, we spread out in groups of two or three.

It was midafternoon when we reached the tan and brown fieldstone building between the highway and Brasstown Creek. The Mountain Valley Cooperative processed dairy and poultry products from the small farms in the area and was owned cooperatively by those who purchased shares in the business. We went inside and looked into the spacious room where milk and cream were separated in huge whirling steel vats. It was immaculately clean, and a strong odor of disinfectant filled the air. In this building butter was churned, ice cream was frozen, and milk was pasteurized and bottled. It was a busy place, with several men hurrying to finish the work so they could go home this Sunday afternoon.

As Monroe joined a man in the doorway to smoke a hand-rolled cigarette, I recognized a familiar face inside and joined Gladys Holland, who was waiting there for her husband, Wayne. Gladys was Miss Gaines's assistant, and Wayne was assistant manager of the Mountain Valley Cooperative. He was supervising the Sunday afternoon activities and would close up when all was in order. As we stood there making small talk, people came in and out for milk, exchanging greetings and family gossip.

After a few minutes, the atmosphere changed abruptly. With each arrival, a newcomer brought an excited version of the news just coming over the radios at home.

"We're at war!"

"They bombed Pearl Harbor!"

"Where's it at?"

The Sunday afternoon gospel music program had been interrupted with the announcement of an attack on Hawaii. None of us knew immediately where Pearl Harbor was, or what was there. I had been so engrossed with my new life in Brasstown that I had given only marginal attention to current affairs in the past three months. As I listened to the sounds of excitement and surprise, I felt an undercurrent of fear flooding from those who were relaying the news. An overwhelming sense of regret and sadness swept over me. Now we were unavoidably involved in World War II.

There could be no question of staying neutral any longer. We had long delayed our formal commitment to the European war. For many years, our country seemed uncertain of our need to become involved in a war on foreign soil. There were many peace marches and a strong America First political movement. In college we read *For Whom the Bell Tolls* and followed the developments of the Spanish Civil War, uncertain of the outcome of the struggle between fascism and communism, but diverted from giving attention to the spread of Nazism. It was a time of uncertainty and unrest. Until German aggression against other countries and mistreatment of Jews became impossible to ignore, it seemed as though we could avoid worldwide involvement. After England and France declared war, our country quietly sent them military supplies, but our government evidently felt they lacked popular support for a "foreign war," so we had remained neutral.

Although I had followed events in Europe, I had been less interested in the international relationships in the Pacific area. Like most Americans, I didn't realize the danger from that direction. Japan's seizure of Manchuria, a province in northern China, had shocked us, but the world was large, and the Far East seemed remote and difficult to understand. Now as we heard the news from the excited radio listeners in Brasstown, it was difficult to comprehend all that had really happened.

It soon became apparent that work at Mountain Valley Creamery was coming to a close for the afternoon. Almost everyone had gone home, eager to get back to safety and their radios. Wayne was ready to lock up. Gladys turned to Monroe and me and said, "Why don't you two come back to the house with Wayne and me, and we can all listen to the radio and find out what is going on?" Wayne seconded her invitation with a characteristic toss of his head, and I looked at Monroe and saw his agreement.

Gladys and Wayne had met as students at the Folk School. Wayne, the eldest in his large family of siblings, grew up in Cherokee County and in 1934, he came to the Folk School as a student. Gladys had come from Hindman School in Kentucky about the same time. In 1940, they were married in a simple garden wedding in front of Mill House. Recently they had built a small rock house on their farm in Brasstown. It sat on the slope overlooking the Hiwassee River, right where the bridge crossed into Cherokee County.

We piled into their dark green pickup truck to ride the three miles back to their house. Gladys squeezed into the middle, and I perched on Monroe's knees with my head touching the roof. As soon as we entered the house, Wayne turned on the radio. Gladys went into her neat little kitchen to put on a pot of coffee, and I followed her. Deftly she fixed a tray with cups and saucers and a plate of homemade cookies and sandwiches. I admired the ease with which she moved. Then we joined the men in the living room. They were sitting in comfortable overstuffed chairs listening to the radio on a small table between them.

The Japanese had attacked units of our Pacific Fleet at the naval base at Pearl Harbor in Hawaii that morning. It was a complete surprise because our Secretary of State was negotiating with Japanese emissaries at the time, so they called it a sneak attack. President Franklin D. Roosevelt had been notified immediately, but so far he had made no public statement.

We listened carefully, but it all seemed far away. I felt so safe here in this charming little pink and blue living room in Brasstown. It was difficult to take this terrible news too seriously. Japan had declared war on the United States, but I was exploring a totally new world, far away from the suburban world of New York City.

In spite of the news, we visited for the rest of the afternoon, not talking much about how it would affect our lives. At last Monroe had to leave to get back to the school to milk the cows, and Wayne offered us both a ride over. I arrived at Farm House in time for supper there. With interest I listened to reactions to the news from Mrs. Campbell and Louise. Although they were surprised at the sudden attack, they were knowledgeable. Pearl Harbor was an important naval base in Hawaii and was surprisingly vulnerable. The Japanese had bombed and sunk many large ships in the harbor. We still didn't have details about the extent of damage and causalities, but our involvement in war was a certainty and a sobering reality.

The next day, the President requested a declaration of war from the Congress, calling December 7, 1941, "a date that will live in infamy." That afternoon the girls at Keith House gathered in small groups, crying and consoling each other as they realized their brothers and boy friends would soon be leaving to go into service. I think they had a much more realistic idea of the four years to come than I had at that time. Neither Monroe nor I had any understanding of the ways in which the war would affect us personally. I had not believed it was necessary for us to go to war. I don't think Monroe had ever considered any part in the military. He was pretty much a homebound mountain man with no longing to see the world. It all seemed too distant from the mountains of Western North Carolina.

Almost immediately, there was a strong reaction in Brasstown toward anything oriental. On several occasions in the past when Mrs. Campbell visited China and Japan, she brought back beautiful household furnishings to enrich and broaden life in this remote corner of Western North Carolina. It was a way of educating students at the Folk School about other parts of the world. She enjoyed the opportunity to keep in touch with friends who had been Christian missionaries in the Far East.

Mrs. Campbell's niece June was married to Harry Cary, the son of missionary parents. He had grown up in Japan before coming to this country to study at Tufts University in Boston.

Harry and June were giving a year of work to the Folk School before starting careers of their own.

Now a whispering wave of gossip and innuendo swept through the school, and Harry was regarded with suspicion. He was a short, sturdily built man with dark hair, but he bore no resemblance to the Japanese people and was in no way related, despite his knowledge of oriental culture. People called him a "nasty Jap" behind his back. Although I doubt if many people in this isolated community had heard the Japanese term hari-kari, which means ritual suicide to avoid disgrace, Harry's name had an unfortunate similarity to the word. Harry was one of the most helpful and best-loved members of the school staff, and he worked with many people in the community.

I had never realized what effect isolation and ignorance have in forming prejudices in people, and how fear turns to anger. This was an insight into human nature that I did not enjoy. Fortunately, the natural courtesy of mountain people restrained the feelings to whispers and snide remarks, but no amount of rational explanation of the truth could erase the underlying feeling of mistrust.

However, life in Brasstown and at the Folk School went on pretty much as usual. One by one, men and boys left the community to join the armed forces. For some it seemed an opportunity to see the world and make a steady income as well as to escape the only world they had known in their lives. But the war was also a golden opportunity to fight for country and justice. There were farewell parties and congratulations, tears, and prayers.

For me nothing appeared to have changed. I was thoroughly involved in the present and the daily chores in shop, farm, house, and school. I had been in Brasstown for little more than three months, and already I was a different person. I was charmed by the personal world of this isolated section of our country. It was so different from the busy and impersonal aspects of New York City and its suburbs. The hope of the economic and social changes that were occurring right here fascinated me more than the rapid alterations in lifestyle that war would soon bring to our country. Little did I realize how drastically this day would shatter my innocence, and how profoundly it would change the lives of all Americans.

A Folk School
Christmas

"We went around the circle giving each person an opportunity to place on the fire one of the decorative evergreen wreaths we had made earlier in the month. . . . We each made a wish for the New Year."

FROM THE SMALL WINDOWS in my snug room at Farm House, I could see the weather vane on the roof of Tower House, above the blacksmith shop. Mrs. Campbell had encouraged Oscar Cantrell, blacksmith extraordinaire, to experiment with the design of wrought iron weather vanes. She hoped to establish a market for them on the coast of Massachusetts where sailors paid close attention to the wind. The silhouetted black cow on top of Tower House stood over a wheel with four spokes pointing north, south, east, and west. A wavering arrow faced into the wind. It was good to know which way the wind was blowing, both literally and metaphorically.

In the weeks of December following Pearl Harbor, the weather turned cooler. A steady northwest wind predicted winter. Each morning I checked to see what the weather promised. Winds of change blew all through our country as people anticipated the upheaval war would bring to our lives. At the Folk School it was no different; subtly we sensed the passing of an era. Monroe shared his perspective on life, a down-to-earth acceptance of daily living, and talking with him enabled me to put aside "causes" and world problems. Small things gave me a sense of security as we heard of former Folk School students signing up for military service. It was at least helpful to know whether the day demanded a sweater or a jacket.

For a while we continued to have warm, sunny days. One Friday when I was doing errands for Miss Gaines in Murphy, I left my tan poplin jacket at the cleaner's. In shirtsleeves and cotton skirt I walked down Hiwassee Street, glorying in the freedom of the sun shining on my bare head even with winter knocking at the door. As the beauty of the mountains captured my spirit, I also found myself comfortable with the intimacy of small towns and fascinated by the whimsical character of the climate here.

However, Christmas was coming. Traditions that marked the season had gradually become part of life here. As the school had grown in the sixteen years since its rudimentary beginning, customs of the mountains were blended with those of its Danish foster country and the Yankee memories of its founders.

Louise told me that December was one of the happiest times of the year at the Folk School. "Most of the students stay through the holidays. At Christmas, each staff family tries to entertain everyone at the school. There are parties in each of the homes on school grounds and in the community. It is a good time to visit around. Why don't you stay for the fun?"

"I don't know," I demurred. "My family always gathers for the holidays. My sister Louise will be home from college, and my older sister, Barbara, and my parents will have a few days off. We enjoy each other and the customs we have had since childhood. No one has ever suggested doing anything else. I don't know what my mother would feel."

"Write and see what your parents think," she suggested.

Within a week, I found my reply on the mail table in Keith House. I was busy and wanted to read the news from home in privacy, so I stuffed the letter in my jacket pocket to read in the evening.

Preparations for Christmas began with the making of wreaths and garlands. Keith House and every building and home was decorated with the harvest of evergreens, pinecones, nuts, and berries from the wealth of the land. One evening we gathered in the Community Room after supper. Staff and former students who lived in the community joined us, but I noticed that Monroe was missing and wondered what he had found better to do.

Murray Martin gathered the inexperienced students around her at a table. Taking a simple ring of heavy wire, she tied pine, spruce, and holly in a full and generous circle, adding pine cones, bright berries, and nuts in bunches, as her artistic spirits dictated. We followed her example. My fingers were all thumbs. The greens definitely had minds of their own, but I struggled on. My first attempt resembled a pine whirligig. I was rewarded with laughter as I held it up for others to see. Murray conceded that it was certainly an original version. The learning group persisted, but I managed to wander to other tables for ideas, jokes, and encouragement. Nevertheless, as the evening wore on, I created several wreaths for Farm House to add to those that Mrs. Campbell and Louise had deftly produced.

The evening came to a close as Mrs. Campbell, Louise, and I decided to call it a night and headed down the path to Farm House. Heady with a sense of accomplishment, we made a strange trio, with our twenty-year gaps in age. My two house-mates sang happily "Here We Go a-Gathering" while I shyly refrained from disturbing the harmony. Back in my room, I sat down on my bed and took the letter from home out of my pocket.

It read: "Dear Ellie, if you would rather stay in Brasstown for Christmas and avoid the long train trip home, Father and I will understand. We'll miss you, of course, but we'll send along a small package and think of you as we celebrate. Love, Mother." It was a warm accepting letter. I stood up and stretched.

Looking out my little windows into the starlit night, I noticed the light on in the upper room of Tower House. Evidently, Monroe was home down there in his bachelor quarters over the blacksmith shop. He was probably reading in front of the big open fire that warmed his room. Often he cooked his own supper there and enjoyed the solitude. I envied his independence, although I loved the sociability of communal living. Impulsively, I gave up the prospect of the long trip home and decided it was time to break the tight-knit family circle. Without further thought, I resolved to spend Christmas in Brasstown and threw myself enthusiastically into all the preparations.

Over a period of several days, enough wreaths were made to decorate every door and every window at Keith House. A huge wreath hung over the fireplace in the Community Room, and a large one decorated the living room fireplace. Garlands festooned the walls. Mistletoe in each doorway and in unexpected places gave Georg the opportunity to tease and kiss "the pretty girls" to his heart's content, amid the laughing admonishments of Marguerite. Even the barns and chicken houses were decorated. We did it all with materials at hand, using the wealth that was ours for the gathering, as contrasted with the artificial world of the "store-bought."

On one special occasion, a huge tree was brought into the Community Room with considerable accompanying excitement.

It almost touched the high rafters. Though it had small electric lights, not candles, the effect was simple. The country was still recovering from the Great Depression, and many mountain homes had little cash to spend on holidays. The Folk School demonstrated how it was possible to use the abundance of nature in the country to make decorations for the tree and the house. Handmade paper lanterns, cranberry wreaths, and strings of cranberries and popcorn, cornucopias, nuts, pinecones, popcorn balls, bright berries, and fruits were easy to collect and decorate.

Soon a contest of sorts was on to find the largest log that could possibly fit into the big fireplace. Georg insisted that Christmas would last as long as the log continued to burn, so we must have a "beeg, *beeg* one." We all laughed with good humor at his myth and teased him in return.

In the kitchen, cookies and cakes and goodies of all sorts were being turned out. The heavy aroma of molasses hung like a cloud above the big wood cookstove. On the small outdoor porch, Helen and Annie Laurie cracked black walnuts. At the high square counter in mid-kitchen, Leila stirred a dozen eggs into a pound cake. Having personally delivered them from the chicken house that morning, I wanted to join the preparations but Miss Gaines shooed me on my way. She was concentrating on the task of teaching the students improved cooking skills and new recipes and didn't consider me a student.

On Saturday night, the girls invited me to join in the candy pulling. They promised that the boys would join us as soon as the candy was ready. Leila measured sorghum into a big heavy pot, added about half as much white sugar, a tablespoon each of butter and vinegar, a pinch of soda, and one of salt. One of the taller girls stirred the mixture on the wood stove until it began to boil. Then she pushed it to the cooler side of the cooking surface and let it cook slowly. We took turns testing a small drop in a cup of cold water until Annie Laurie finally held up a sample that was crisp. It had reached the soft crack stage. Miss Gaines poured it out on a large marble slab as we watched.

Patiently we waited while it cooled, chattering and giggling in anticipation as a few of the boys sauntered in to join us. When the taffy was manageable, we buttered our hands. Leila Stalcup, the leader of the fun that evening, called for volunteers "with tough hands." Of course I wanted to show off by having the toughest hands. We patted the candy into soft mounds. Then Ves, Annie Laurie, and I each picked up a big ball of the hot sweet. Moving it gingerly back and forth between hands, we stretched it into a short rope. Then they each handed one end to Clyde and Claude, Leila's brothers.

I tossed my end to Monroe. He and I expanded it between us until we had to double it over to keep it from sagging to the floor. We stretched it again, pulling it ever thinner and lighter, until the dark brown became a pale taffy color, pencil thin. Then almost cold and becoming stiff, it was cut into short pieces. Ready for eating, the delicious, mellow sticky sweetness of the taffy melted in our mouths with the promise of Christmas to come. According to custom, a few of the girls offered their strings to a boyfriend. Each started eating the sweet confection at the opposite end, meeting in the middle with a kiss. I was tempted, but Muns didn't offer to demonstrate so neither did I.

A week or two before Christmas, the Brasstown Women's Club gave a party for all the "Old Folks" living in the country-side surrounding the community. I still didn't know many people in Brasstown, but this gave me a glimpse of how families here took care of each other and worked together for their community.

On several occasions during the autumn months, Louise Pitman took me to visit in homes within walking distance of the school. The Caldwell family of seven lived in the house right next to Quedor's Store at the corner of Brasstown Road and U.S. Highway 64. One afternoon after work, Louise and I stopped in to visit Quedor's wife, Lillian, who had named her only daughter Louise. The two women began talking about the Brasstown Women's Club.

"You know we're planning to have the Old Folks' Party at the school again this year," Lillian said.

"That's good," Louise agreed. "It always means so much to all those women who don't get out very often, especially those up Little Brasstown and over on Pine Log. What can I do to help?"

"You usually type out the invitations. Reckon you can do that again? Harry Cary used to pick up some of the folks who have too far to walk and haven't got a ride. I guess he'll do that again. Quedor will give out the stick candy, and he'll get some oranges if they have them when he goes to Atlanta," Lillian said.

She was a rather tall woman, heavy in middle age after bearing five young'uns. She had a pleasant smile and blue eyes that crinkled with friendliness. Louise and she continued to plan, reminiscing about past years, and speculating about who in the community could provide talent for entertainment.

On the walk back home, Louise and I talked about the folks they would invite. "Do you know what we mean by 'old folks'?" she asked. "It includes anyone over sixty who lives in the Brasstown community."

Sensing my surprise and curiosity, she continued, "Life isn't easy here. Many people work so hard that they are ready to rest by the time they reach sixty. They're isolated, too, especially the women, who are the backbone of rural life. For a successful farm, a man relies a great deal on the cooperation, skill, and talent of his wife, as well as on her good health and ability to produce small laborers to help on the farm. Most of the women don't drive. They don't get out unless their husbands take them. Everyone enjoys the Old Folks' Party. It's a special occasion to bring together old friends who don't see each other as often as they'd like. They've known each other all their lives, but don't see each other regularly and hardly ever get together unless it's for a funeral. So, the Women's Club has a great project. They know that the women need to see each other once in a while, especially at Christmas time."

In that way I was more or less prepared for the party. It was a wonderful event. The school provided plenty of music with the piano to set the mood as people gathered. A number of men brought fiddles. There were opportunities for performance by anyone willing to show off a talent. Uncle Bill Clayton and Wade Beach buck danced in the old mountain style, and any of the other old-timers who wanted to compete met the challenge and joined in. Mae Scroggs told tall tales, and Alla Scroggs told jokes. Each person's contribution to the entertainment was met with laughter, applause, and merriment. It was a revelation to me to see grown people enjoying themselves in the simple pleasures of being together, quite different from the dinner or cocktail parties that my parents and friends attended occasionally. There the conversation was polite and formal; here everyone exchanged family news, jokes, and stories, ready for a good time.

On Christmas Eve, everyone in the community was invited to a nativity play enacted by the students and performed on the low platform in the Community Room. Mrs. Campbell wrote, directed, and coached it. Each year she modified the script to accommodate the talent and the number of students who would participate. This year I could tell she was disappointed that no one had an exceptionally gifted solo voice. However, she managed to assemble a complete cast in spite of the small student body, and they all enjoyed taking a part.

Traditional folk carols were included in the evening program, and everyone was encouraged to join the singing. "The Cherry Tree Carol," an old folk tune that was well known in England and recently discovered in both Clay County and in Murphy, was sung by Bert Smith, who came in on leave from military service at the last moment. I had never heard this beautiful carol sung. It tells the story about Joseph, the expectant Mary, and the cherry tree that bowed down to give her fruit. I was delighted and charmed by it. "Brightest and Best," a Kentucky folk carol, and "The Twelve Days of Christmas" also appeared to be favorites. Following the play, the caroling, and the dancing, we gathered around the tree. There were small gifts for everyone who had come to the program although the Folk School family saved their gifts for each other for Old Christmas on January 6.

After the excitement of the Christmas celebration, each household entertained all the young people and students at their individual houses. Murray and Dub Martin had remodeled an old mountain house on a farm adjoining Folk School land. With her artistic talent, Murray had created a glorious collection of mountain craftwork. She and Dub had papered the rough wooden walls with small-flowered insulating wallpaper in the two front rooms. They made a charming backdrop for antique rockers, a high four-poster bed with handwoven coverlet, rag rugs on the floor, and carvings on a high shelf. Three oil lamps had been adapted for electricity. Chicken feed sack curtains hung at both windows. The kitchen was furnished with wormy chestnut cabinets that Dub had made in the Folk School shop. Murray served hot chocolate with marshmallows and fresh baked sugar cookies. We played old-time games like Blind Man's Buff and Pin the Tail on the Reindeer, way into the night.

Another evening Harriet and Gwen Cornwell invited everyone over to Brasstown to the new house they had recently built and were in the process of completing. Gwen had set up incubators in the full basement of the house and was going into the hatchery business as a sideline to his farming. Harriet was a charming hostess, bustling around to make everyone feel at home. She had set up card tables in the living room in front of the huge stone fireplace for a simple supper. Each table was set with four places on a gingham tablecloth. Candles in handmade iron candlesticks were in the center of every table, and at each place was a small favor. As I had recently begun to knit a sweater for Bundles for Britain, my favor was a small china figurine of a girl knitting a blue ball of yarn. Afterwards Harriet played the upright piano and we all sang Christmas carols for a rousing good time.

There was a party every night until New Year's and then a special celebration at Mill House. The boys' dormitory was located in the half of Mill House where the mill wheel turned. Marguerite and Georg lived in the other half. The Bidstrups' half was tiny and charmingly decorated in Scandinavian style. The front door was divided in a way that allowed the top half to be open while the lower half remained closed. There was a small entry with a wrought iron rack for wraps and each of the wooden doors had ornamental iron hinges and latches. A tiny kitchen with quaint high windows made wonderful use of every inch of space with small appliances and cabinets that fit neatly into each corner.

The living room had a small plaster-sealed fireplace in which a fire burned cheerily. All the furniture was handmade and the curtains handwoven. In one corner of the cozy room, an iron spiral staircase, painted red, twisted up to a sitting room, bedroom, and bath under the eaves. Marguerite served mulled cider, crackers and cheese, and Scandinavian cookies of all sorts. Of course, there was marzipan, the Danish candy, and popcorn balls for everyone.

We had a wonderful time at those Christmas parties. Finally, for Old Christmas on January 6, we commemorated the coming of the Wise Men with a last party and the telling of tales in the living room at Keith House. Then the Folk School family exchanged a few gifts. Louise gave me a handwrought, pewter napkin ring. We had drawn names and usually exchanged with only one person, however Miss Gaines gave me a small Blenko glass vase. She had ordered several earlier in the fall and over-looked it in unpacking the carton. Later she had given the box to the craft shop, and I found the vase among the packing material and took it back to her. She rewarded me with it as a gift. There were no other presents, but there were many Christmas wishes and much good cheer.

In the circle around the open fire, we sang carols: "Go Tell It on the Mountain," "I Wonder as I Wander," "There Were Three Ships," and "We Three Kings," among others. We each chose a favorite. When the fire died down somewhat, we went around the circle giving each person an opportunity to place on the fire one of the decorative evergreen wreaths we had made earlier in the month. The room was fragrant with the pungency of pine and fir and spruce, still fresh enough to fill the air. Carefully in turn, we placed our offerings on the coals. With a rush of sound and a shower of sparks, the fire flared as we each made a wish for the New Year. My wish for the coming year was for peace and happiness for the Folk School family.

The Challenge

Photo courtesy of the John C. Campbell Folk School Archives, Brasstown, North Carolina.

"I went up to Little Brasstown Baptist Church regularly. . . . The love of God and my need for fellowship drew me to the little church."

AFTER THE HOLIDAY WAS OVER, I was glad that I had stayed in Brasstown for Christmas. The celebrations gave me a sense of traditions in the making. Parties in the community hinted at the possibility of social life beyond the Folk School family. I was eager to know more and to expand my sense of belonging. The nativity play and the singing of carols at the school helped me realize the importance of faith in the country, something I had hitherto taken for granted. I was interested in knowing more about the relationship of the school's values to those of the community. A few months after I settled at the Folk School, Louise invited me to go to church with her.

"Where do you go to church?" I asked.

"Usually we go up to Little Brasstown Baptist Church," she replied.

Little Brasstown Baptist Church stands in a clearing on the side of the hill above the Folk School. In 1941, it was a one-room white clapboard building, a guardian of righteousness welcoming the folks of the community from near and far. I had never attended a Baptist church, so I was curious to know what kind of service drew people to this small building set apart from other structures in the community.

Louise's invitation surprised me because I noticed that the Folk School staff carefully avoided discussing specific aspects of religion or politics. I knew that most of the teachers had strong opinions and beliefs, and I was well aware of the differences between religious beliefs and practices in the North and those in the South. I thought it was probably wise of the staff not to hurt feelings or encourage controversy. Although I had always gone to church regularly at home and in college, I didn't really expect to go to church in Brasstown. Upon the advice of my senior college professor, when I came to the mountains I had brought with me my King James Version of the Bible.

Yankee or Southerner, we did have a safe common ground in the Bible. No matter how much we avoided discussions of religious topics, God's Word provided solid material for study and a reason to attend church. Both Marguerite and Mrs. Campbell occasionally taught Sunday School at Little Brasstown. Herman Estes was devout in attendance there. Each week he strode purposefully up the path toward the church, his dog-eared Bible held lovingly under one arm.

Louise's invitation to services pleased me. Cautiously she asked me a bit about my religious background. Her questions caused me to reflect on my spiritual journey to that point. It began as an infant when I was baptized in the Dutch Reformed Church of my ancestors on Fifth Avenue in New York City. It continued when I was a child with occasional church attendance and training in prayer at home. During my three years at an Episcopal college preparatory school, I grew spiritually, became serious in my search for the truth in God, and decided to be confirmed in my faith.

During my college years, I avidly searched other traditions. I was particularly attracted to reflections on religious values in English literature, in history, and in sociology. I attended many different churches in the town of Poughkeepsie as well as chapel on the college campus. We heard visiting preachers from leading churches of New York City, and I reported on them for the Poughkeepsie newspaper. My senior thesis in the contemporary press course examined the relationship between individual freedom of thought and the ways in which personal values are influenced by society. I left college with a strong sense that the meaning of life lay in one's ability to influence the lives of other people.

I had no idea what I could do in the way of work with people, but I was ready to learn as much as I could about life in Brasstown and the possibilities there. I wanted to explore different ideas and ways of worship. Louise tried to prepare me for a new experience by telling me that country church services in the South were different from any I had attended before. She assured me that everyone dressed simply. The next Sunday, Louise stopped by Keith House so that I could walk up to church with her.

Like the students and others who chose to go to church, we headed up a narrow, winding path behind the school lumberyard to Little Brasstown Baptist Church. As we climbed the hill, I remembered Saint John's Episcopal Church of my childhood. How I hated to walk in with my family after the service had started. I felt every eye upon us as we tried to find places in the prayer book or hymnal. That old fear returned on my first Sunday in Brasstown. I hoped we wouldn't be late, or worse, conspicuous. Shy misgivings assailed me.

When Louise and I reached the top of the path, many people had already gathered in the clearing around the church, talking together in small groups. A few cars and pickup trucks were parked off to the side, mostly Fords and Chevrolets and one Model A, but most people walked to services from several miles away. There was no sense of urgency, nor was there any scheduled time for things to begin. A pleasant air of anticipation seemed to pervade the gathering.

First Louise introduced me to several of the older women in a group. Then a tall man in clean starched overalls with a wide-brimmed black hat rang a large brass bell hanging from a wooden trestle. It was a signal to start moving inside. Low-backed wooden benches flanked both sides of the central aisle. The tall man removed his hat, ushered us in, and took his place up front. Louise whispered to me that it was the man everyone called Uncle Bill Clayton.

The church filled up quickly. Most men sat on the right side, some still wearing sweat-stained fedoras pushed back on their heads or slanted rakishly over one eye. The elders of the congregation had removed their hats and held them in their laps or hung them on a pegboard as they came through the front door.

Women sat together on the left side of the room, the older ones in "Sunday dresses" and hats. The younger women held lap babies too young to walk and cradled babes in arms. Toddlers sat shyly by their mothers or escaped to wander up and down the aisle. Teenagers chose their places in the back pews from whence drifted occasional subdued giggles.

At the front, facing the congregation, a woman sat at an upright piano. She leaned forward and began pounding out "The Little Brown Church in the Vale" on the keys. Everyone sang the familiar tune, but I didn't know it or the other songs.

The old hymns that had become part of my very being in boarding school and in the familiar churches of my previous life were not part of the repertoire here. I longed for the familiar measures of "Faith of Our Fathers," or "Rock of Ages," but contemporary songs with religious themes and a catchy rhythm were more popular. I was introduced to a song about calling Jesus on the telephone. There seemed to be a genuine effort to make the message meaningful to modern ears.

After the singing there was an interim. People chatted, greeting each other, catching up on news from those they hadn't seen recently, inquiring about the health of people who had been sick. Several people walked up and down the aisle, in and out the front door. A stray dog wandered in when the door was left open and was greeted by laughter and embarrassed caresses from his small owner, who then dragged him out by the collar. After a while, some of the men and all of the boys went outside.

After a reasonable recess, Uncle Bill called the congregation to order with a prayer. It was a fervent, freewheeling intercessory prayer that covered personal concerns for the health of individual members not able to come to church, a petition for seasonable weather, and a plea for an inspired message from a preacher this morning. Uncle Bill concluded with thanksgiving for the many blessings we had received. His prayer was punctuated from time to time with "amens" from different voices.

Almost immediately, another gentleman stood up and announced that there would be preaching this morning, "as soon as the preacher can get here." He passed a hat so there would be money to pay the preacher. Then the hat was passed again for money to care for a sick member of the congregation. Repeated collections helped provide for the maintenance of the church: the light bill, transportation for the preacher, coal for the stove, and more. Each time, members emptied pockets, grumbled with good nature, and giggled in embarrassment. Leaders met this with eloquent exhortations and spontaneous prayers for meeting each need. Finally, those who were responsible for the care of the church were satisfied.

While we waited, the congregation divided into groups for Sunday school. The young people and children gathered in the front pews. A teacher told the story of Noah and the ark. She put in all the details of the building of the vessel, its measurements, the size of the interior, the kind of wood Noah used, and so forth. Then she drew a word picture of the rain and the terror of the flood. She ended by describing the animals, listing those that were familiar here in the mountains and the exotic ones best known from elsewhere. I was impressed with her story-telling skills and ability to keep the interest of her listeners of all ages.

In conclusion, she asked each of us to recite a Bible verse. The small children were ready with a verse, but I became anxious and dry-mouthed. I was afraid I didn't know scripture by heart as well as most folks did. However, I was relieved as I listened to the brief verses of the big overgrown boys. Red-faced with eyes downcast, one mumbled, "Jesus wept." Another smiled. "God is love," he said as he glanced sidewise at the row of girls across from him. Relieved that their answers were simple, I managed to make a reply. "In the beginning God created the heavens and the earth." Then the bell rang again, and adults returned to fill the church. It was time for the sermon.

Mountain preaching was new to me. A small stoutly built man greeted us and apologized for his tardiness. He had had car trouble. He drew a big breath and began, intoning in a deep voice, "My message for the day is Salvation."

I had seen banners reading "Jesus Saves" stretched across narrow valleys in Kentucky when we had driven through the mountains the previous spring. Outside of Murphy on the side of the highway was a stone cross with the message, "Jesus is coming soon." However, I was not prepared for the fervent, enthusiastic message with which he intended to shape listeners into righteous behavior by arousing fear of hellfire and damnation. I was glad to be sitting again with Louise and the older women. They seemed unperturbed, but I was amazed at the words and the emotion with which they were delivered. The congregation listened to the message with appreciation, punctuating it with an occasional "amen." The sermon held little meaning for me, and the emotion was frightening.

The excitement at Little Brasstown Church that morning reminded me of my feelings when I had visited Father Divine's mission in Harlem as part of a college course in Christianity and the Social Order. An evangelical preacher of considerable success, Father Divine introduced many people in New York to the Gospel of Jesus Christ during the difficult years of the Great Depression. By God's grace, his mission gave food, clothing, shelter, and the word of God to many African Americans in that part of the city. People at the mission welcomed our college class with friendly informality. After introductions and a tour of the old brownstone house where they provided services, we sat down to dinner. The huge table filled the small room, and we crowded elbow to elbow in a sea of dark-skinned people of all ages. Bowls of turnip greens, fried chicken, mashed potatoes, yams, and applesauce were passed from person to person, and each guest helped himself. The sense of community was strong. Despite very different people and a totally different environment at Brasstown, I found there again the same sort of genuine worshipping community.

Subsequently, I went up to Little Brasstown Baptist Church regularly. I had always enjoyed going to church, and Sunday seemed empty without an opportunity to worship. Church was a great place to get to know young people in the community. At the school, Sunday was a day apart. Nothing much was expected from me, so the love of God and my need for fellowship drew me to the little church. After experiencing Christmas at the Folk School, I was even more eager to understand how country faith was shaped in this church. Usually after the sermon, we young singles left the pews for the older people and went outside to discuss the sermon and other matters of common interest. We sat on a fallen tree and a couple of improvised benches made of rough boards laid across fallen logs. Socializing was in order, but often the conversation took a Biblical turn.

I knew when I had left the intellectual environment of college to come to the Appalachian Mountains that I was entering the Bible Belt. Although I knew very well what I believed, I felt ill prepared and too shy to quote from the Bible so I didn't enter into religious discussion when it turned serious. As the winter progressed and we began to get better acquainted, there was talk of baptism in the spring.

"Will there be a special service?" I asked innocently.

"Of course. It's always in Brasstown Creek as soon as the weather is warm."

"What do you mean, 'as soon as the weather is warm'?" I asked, totally mystified.

"You know. There has to be running water deep enough to dunk the person under. In the winter the water is too cold for that, so we wait for the water to warm up a bit. Probably on the first sunny Sunday in the spring, there'll be preaching down at the creek and a baptism."

"Who'll be baptized?"

"You'll see. Anyone who gets saved that day."

"Really?"

That elicited a question for which I was totally unprepared. A tall young teenager challenged me, "Are you saved?"

Taken off guard, I asked, "What do you mean?"

They attempted to explain by asking, "Have you been born again?"

"What do you mean 'born again'?"

They asked again, "Are you saved?"

Then several of the young people who had gathered told me emphatically, "If you have to ask, you surely haven't been saved!"

Awkwardly and defensively, I tried to explain without any real idea of what they were asking. "I was baptized when I was a baby and confirmed when I was sixteen. Certainly, I believe in Jesus, God, and the Holy Spirit. Is that what you are asking? Is that what you mean by being 'saved'?"

No one would answer. No one would listen. They had no interest in theological discussions, in the Trinity, Incarnation, and the Resurrection. I felt as if no one there believed that I had been saved.

"What do they think I need to be saved from?" I wondered silently, completely confused by the personal use of the expression.

I had been raised to believe trustingly in a loving God to whom I could turn in prayer at any time. Every night of my life, I asked forgiveness of the mistakes I had made that day. Each morning I tried again to follow the teachings of Jesus Christ. I had never been taught to fear God or to feel the danger of Hell. I trusted God completely with my life and always wanted to please Him. What did I need to be saved from?

Slowly it dawned on me that here was a misunderstanding I could not change. My experiences and those of the Brasstown faithful were too different to stand on the common ground of understanding. I really wanted to belong in that group of young people, so after my initial response, I accepted their questions as a challenge for me to understand rather than as an attack on my faith.

On subsequent Sundays, I listened carefully to the recitations of Bible verses, to the teaching, to the questions and answers of the adults in Sunday School classes, and to the "preaching." It was no use. My beliefs were very different from what I was hearing, but I didn't want to question theirs. Slowly the words of the songs began to give me an understanding of the ways in which religion influenced life in the mountains.

Although I could appreciate the sincerity of these young people in Brasstown and even share their feelings, they used words so different from those with which I understood my own faith in God that the spiritual gap between us was too wide to cross.

No one invited me to attend the baptism later that spring, and I was acutely aware of the religious gulf that separated me from my friends and co-workers. I gained some understanding that God reaches out to each of us in different ways, and although I was comforted by that thought, I continued to feel distant and isolated in matters of religion.

One Sunday afternoon after that challenge, I asked Monroe if he had been saved. He laughed, "Of course, I have. I was almost drowned in Hemptown Creek, when I was just twelve years old."

"Is that what you mean by 'saved'? Is it the same as deciding to be baptized or joining the church?"

"Pretty much so. We had a big revival at the church that spring. We always had services at either the Methodist or the Baptist Church. They are right across the highway from each other in Hemptown, so we just visited back and forth, a different church each Sunday. The year I was twelve, the revival was at the Baptist Church. After the preaching when the call came to come forward if we believed in God, I went right up. Afterward I was baptized, but I joined the Methodist Church because my father was Superintendent of Sunday School there."

"Why don't you ever go to church here?" I asked.

"Well I do sometimes, but we don't usually get through milking and all in time for me to get there often. Anyway, we went to church so much when I was home that I never really got used to going up here. Every Sunday Dad would bring the preacher home with him after the service. By the time they ate all the good pieces of chicken Mother fried for dinner each week, I was lucky to get the gizzard. I've always liked the gizzard, and I still go to church sometimes."

I told him about the challenge at Little Brasstown and how I'd been baptized as a baby and joined the church when I was sixteen. Monroe smiled and reassured me. "Don't worry about what they said. If you've been baptized and believe in Jesus, you've been saved. You're all right."

It was at Little Brasstown Baptist Church in 1942 that I broadened my Christian perspective and engaged my mind in studying the Bible. It was an important step in my lifelong search for understanding of how Christians share common ground. In different denominations and walks of life, we use a variety of ways to express our faith in God through worship and in our lives.

Winter
in the Mountains

Daisy Dame. Photo courtesy of the John C. Campbell Folk School Archives, Brasstown, North Carolina.

"I dearly loved the old rooms, the wide-board floors, . . . but it was, of course, Mrs. Campbell who made it a home."

WINTER IN THE MOUNTAINS was a time to look inward, for settling in. For me it was the season when I began to understand the depth of life offered in the country: pleasure in the beauty of each day, rewards that come in caring for animals, friendships formed with such a variety of people, the simple joy of companionship.

Denuded of their leaves, the hardwoods studded the ridges, revealing the strong outlines of the close hills and the more distant peaks. Whenever weather permitted, I sat on the steps leading down from Keith House and looked toward the mountains beyond the small scattered cluster of Brasstown houses and stores. The mountains symbolized for me the backbone and vision of the pioneers of the last century. I continued to marvel at the courage and determination of those settlers who followed waterways and Indian trails to make new lives for themselves in this beautiful country.

At the Folk School, classes took on serious importance, as the time spent on farm work was less intense. Instructional classes in farm bookkeeping, nutrition, health, homemaking and current events were held during the day. There were conversations about books, debates about ways that democracy can function smoothly, and stories about the history of Appalachia.

Farm work in winter was also different. Now the primary work was maintenance. Cows had to be fed and milked, chickens watered and fed, and eggs gathered. Men and boys at the school and in the community felled trees in the woods with triumphant shouts of "timber!" When they were working near the shop, I took a break and went out to watch. A stalwart person at each end of a long crosscut saw divided the trunks into fireplace-length logs while another man deftly split them into halves or quarters with an ax. They cut the smaller trees and large branches into shorter lengths to burn in the cookstoves and heaters. Georg took time to teach the boys how to stack firewood in a picturesque Scandinavian rounded cone that shed rain. "It vill look better in your farmyard that vay," he urged. After the first morning spent in the woods, the six boys came to Keith House for dinner as tired and satisfied as a winning basketball team.

In each of the houses, we enjoyed the warmth of open fires in living rooms. At Keith House the heat of the big wood furnace in the basement and the comfort of the iron cookstove in the kitchen made life cozy. There was plenty of wood for all the houses on the school grounds. The boys delivered it to the residences at Farm House, Mill House, Hill House, Pine View Cottage, and Rock House, as well as to Keith House.

In the evenings after supper, classes in different crafts were offered, and I was welcome to join them. Murray Martin taught carving in the large room at the top of the stairs in Keith House as the overhead light that hung from the ceiling there was brighter than in any other room. We sat around a table under the light in the straight, wooden chairs that the citizens of Brasstown had made for the school during its early years. Some chairs were more comfortable than others, but they all had straight backs, made to keep us at attention. Each of us had an apron or a page of the *Asheville Citizen* covering our laps to catch the carving scraps. Murray carved as she taught. In her hand was a block of white holly that she was shaping into the figure of a cherub for a Christmas crèche.

Several of the students were quite talented with their jackknives. We could choose pieces of wood from the shop that had already been sawed in the rough outlines of various animals. Around the table, each person worked with a block and a sharp penknife. Over the next several weeks, our carvings took shape. I remember Barry's carving that looked like Georg's big shaggy black collie, Jack. We all loved that school mascot, who followed Georg everywhere and waited patiently for him wherever he was.

Several of the girls were carving napkin rings in the shapes of squirrels, rabbits, or cats. I selected a cherry wood block to carve a cocker spaniel. Months earlier when I came to Brasstown in September, I had left a charming golden-haired spaniel puppy at home with my sister Louise. It had been a birthday present for her from a farm kennel in Maine the previous summer. She named him Mr. Chips and left him with Mother when she went back to college in the fall. The memory of Mr. Chips made me a bit homesick so I thought I would carve his likeness as a surprise gift for Louise when I went back home.

At first in carving class, we each rounded out our carving roughly with brave strokes of our knives. As the carving took shape, Murray made suggestions to help us get a lifelike look. For several evenings I carved quietly, whittling away happily and observing the progress of others as I tried to shape my block to look like Chipsie. Finally, I held my work up for Murray to see.

"It doesn't look like a cocker spaniel," I complained, self-critically.

"No wonder it doesn't," Murray said bluntly. "You chose a hound block. You can't make it look like a cocker spaniel."

I laughed and considered her suggestion that I carve a foxhound from that block, but I lost heart. I was embarrassed by my mistake, and I didn't want to carve something my sister wouldn't recognize. I discovered carving was hard work. Like an icy shower, Murray's remark was sufficiently disappointing and discouraging to lead me to spend time on different crafts. Occasionally that winter, I would drop in on the carving class as the others progressed. I watched them use sandpaper to smooth away the knife marks and round the carvings, but I never resumed my ambition to carve. For many years I kept the rough beginning of a foxhound as a reminder to appreciate the fine carvings that others seemed to do so easily and well.

My adventures in the woodworking class were more successful. Some evenings Herman Estes taught at the woodworking shop, and during the year almost every student made a footstool. Some had carved tops and others had seats of woven corn shucks. The shucks, peeled from dried ears of corn, were dampened and twisted together into a thin rope. Then the rope was woven back and forth between the top rungs of the stool to form a low seat or footrest. Another favorite woodworking project was a hanging shelf for "whatnots."

Monroe told me that since his first year at the Folk School in 1937, he had made at least one of each of the projects and had given them to his family and friends.

"Have you ever made a real table?" I asked him.

"I started a round table last year," he said, "but I never finished it."

"Well, why don't you finish it now?" I asked.

"No, I don't want to, but you can finish it if you want to, and it will be yours," he offered.

I accepted the offer. The piece was a round table on a pedestal. The top was complete with rounded edges and sanded top. The four curved legs were already shaped, and the tenons were cut to fit into the pedestal, but the pedestal itself, although turned and shaped, was waiting for the finishing touch. I needed to cut grooves, called fluting, in the long rounded curve of the shaft. When I told Herman I wanted to work on the table and finish the fluting, he shook his head in disbelief.

"You can't possibly do that. The machines are dangerous, and girls never use the one that cuts the fluting," he said firmly. "You'll get hurt."

"I can do it if you'll show me how," I insisted.

He shook his head and pushed his cap further back on his head.

"Please, Herman, I know I can do it." I waited. He went on helping the others in the class. Finally, he came back to me.

"I can't show you while I'm teaching the rest of this class. If you have time tomorrow morning, I'll show you how to use the machine when I have a chance."

I grinned thankfully and didn't bother him any more that evening. The next morning when I had finished preparing the packages that needed to go out in the afternoon mail, I went into the woodshop. Herman was standing at the lathe. He had placed my pedestal in the vise to hold it so I could lower it through the knives to cut the fluting. He explained how to pull the lever down very slowly. Then he stepped away and busied himself with his back to me as if he couldn't bear to watch.

With a tremendous sense of power, I carefully followed his instructions and watched the lines cut into the round pedestal. I steadied the piece with my right hand on the base and rejoiced in the process that looked so precise and perfect. A sharp nick on the index finger of my right hand humbled me. I had held my hand too close to the sharp, whirring knives. I pulled the switch on the machine and drew back quickly, putting my hand in my jacket pocket. I was more afraid that Herman would see what I had done than I was afraid of the pain.

"Does that look all right?" I called to Herman.

"I'll be swanny," he exclaimed, "that's great. I'll take it out of the vise for you."

"Thank you. I need to get back to work. I'll see you later. Thanks a lot, Herman. That was fun."

Pushing my clenched fist and bleeding finger deep in my pocket, I escaped to the bathroom and ran icy cold water over the cut until I could wrap it in a paper towel and return to the office. I knew if Herman saw what had happened, he'd never allow me to use the machines again.

As days went by, I put the table together, glued and sanded it all, and finished it with multiple coats of shellac, buffed to a soft sheen with fine steel wool. Herman was as proud of my accomplishment as I, and he never questioned my willingness to work in the shop again. Although the table was always my most adventurous project, Herman remained a lifelong friend and consultant.

The library at Keith House was open for community readers as well as students, especially during the winter while everyone had time for relaxation. That year under Harry Cary's sponsorship, we also had movies, rented from a mail order service. The Folk School Community Room was more accessible for many than Murphy's Henn Theatre eight miles away, so neighbors were welcomed and were asked for a small fee to offset the cost of the film.

To the whirring sound of 16mm reels, we saw such classics as *All Quiet on the Western Front*. Cowboy westerns were favored, and occasionally there was a comedy. At lunch one day, Harry promised a real treat; Charlie Chaplin in *City Lights* was the film of the evening. To Harry's surprise, the Brasstown audience and Folk School students gave it poor reviews. The silent comedy was not as well received as the usual slapstick, or Laurel and Hardy. Perhaps I sensed a bit of cultural dissonance, but it didn't bother me or discourage Harry's choices.

In my free time, I liked to visit with June Cary at Pine View Cottage down the road from the barns. June and Harry had two little boys: their infant, Richard, and Loren, who was two. June painted and designed furniture to be made to her scale drawings by students or by the woodworking shop. One of her most popular designs was a nest of tables that proved to be a popular best seller. She had also designed a comfortable low chair with a seat and back upholstered in handwoven wool. Her twin beds had cherry head- and footboards laced with twisted corn shucks. Although she used traditional designs, much of her work had an original sense about it.

June also taught painting and drawing to the students. With June's encouragement, some of them painted beautiful scenes of the local countryside. Earlier that year I had seen Fannie Kate Brendle's example of work that would enrich her home for years to come. Many other students took paintings home with them when they left the school. As the painting students were mostly girls, the boys liked to tease them about their newfound interest in nature. "That sunset is so beautiful. I'd just like to paint it," became a joking remark among those who liked poking fun at anything serious or anything girls especially enjoyed learning.

June had grown up in the suburbs of Boston. When not busy with the boys and her work for the school, she painted landscapes in oil on canvas. They were mountain scenes or views of some of the houses at the Folk School. Sometimes she painted scenes that she remembered from Nantucket, where she and I both had spent summers during childhood. June probably would have preferred to spend her time pursuing a career in art, but found herself following in family footsteps as she volunteered to teach mountain young people. She and Harry were giving two years of their lives to help Mrs. Campbell establish the Folk School. June was not the only one of her family to be part of the experiment in mountain living; her parents were on the school's board of directors. Her sister Olive had spent a year here. June's brother, Brad Coolidge, and his wife, Jean, were also part of the Folk School for many, many years.

June was glad to have a woman from a Yankee background with whom to share impressions. It was a welcome change of pace for me also. I helped her as she dealt with diapers, laundry, bottles, feeding times, and the challenges of a home heated with only a wood cookstove and a couple of small fireplaces.

One afternoon she greeted me with a request, "Would you take a picture of Loren's legs? He is somewhat bow-legged and the pediatrician who saw him when we visited my parents at Christmas wanted to see how well his legs are straightening." I was glad to take my camera down on my next free afternoon. When word came back several weeks later from the pediatrician that Loren's legs appeared to be straighter, I was pleased and June was thankful. I knew that June longed to return to Boston, and that she worried about the lack of medical specialists for her children locally.

Usually toward the end of my visit, June disappeared into the kitchen while I watched the boys. Soon I heard the cheerful whistle of the teakettle. The smoky smell of Lapsang souchong tea preceded her as she came back to the dining table with a tray laden with handle-free oriental cups and a basket of shortbread cookies.

Harry continued to be actively involved in school publicity and community relationships, the library, and student recruitment. Each of the Carys taught a class for Folk School students and acted as informal counselors. Nevertheless, they always made time for me. It was good to have friends who knew the New England environment that I loved as part of my youth. Conversations with both June and Harry helped me see mountain life in perspective and gain a sense of the early years of the Folk School as they saw it through family eyes.

Sometimes after a good visit and a cup of hot tea with June and her little ones, I went on to the milking barn on my way back up the hill to Farm House. It was familiar territory. On Sunday afternoons it was not unusual for some of the Folk School girls to walk down to the barns to watch the milking and hurry the work along so that the boys could join in any extracurricular activities that were taking place that evening. I often went along, and I soon became comfortable with the rich odor of cow manure and the warm smell of fresh milk.

As my visits became routine, I often helped in the work. Some of the cows were milked by hand. I learned that when a cow is cut by barbed wire or has mastitis and fever in the udder, she needs individual attention, and some cows have temperaments that respond better to hand milking. One day Monroe suggested that I try hand milking. I sat down on the milking stool, grasped the warm teats in each fist, and squeezed. They were firmer than I had imagined and only a drop or two emerged, despite my best effort.

"Let me show you," my mentor offered and demonstrated by directing a brisk flow into the bucket. At first the steady stream zinged resoundingly into the emptiness with the crescendo diminishing as the bucket filled with pungent, foaming liquid.

Most of the herd was machine-milked, however. The stainless steel vacuum milking machine was attached to a pipe running along the top of the frame holding the stanchions. The machine had a lid from which four hoses with teat cups led to the cow's udder. The pump, attached to the pipe overhead, formed a vacuum so that the cups drew the milk into the bucket. With just a switching of the tail and an occasional stamping of the foot, most of the cows suffered the indignity of machine milking.

As each animal was relieved, I helped carry the milk to the milk room. There we weighed the bucket on the hanging scale, recorded the amount on the chart on the wall, and then poured the milk through the filter-lined strainer into a ten-gallon milk can. Milking complete, two boys swung the milk cans across the tiny bridge and into the springhouse.

In the springhouse, the milk cans were placed in the cement trough filled with ice-cold water that ran from the mountain spring above into the branch below. After the next morning's milking, the cool milk of the previous night and the fresh milk of the morning were loaded on the school pickup truck and delivered to the Mountain Valley Creamery for separating, pasteurizing, and bottling in glass pints and quarts.

The cows fascinated me. Studying the history of art in school, I had admired the pastoral landscapes of English artists of the nineteenth century. I considered cows the most peaceful of animals. Their calm acceptance of life was a quality I envied. I found that each cow had a personality, and many were fractious. Nevertheless, the milking process held genuine appeal for me.

Usually before I returned to Farm House, I fed the chickens and collected the eggs. We had Rhode Island reds that provided plenty of eggs for the school and a surplus to sell to the Mountain Valley Cooperative. Georg told me that the reds were a good choice because unlike the white Leghorns, another primarily egg-producing breed, the reds were plump and made good roast or stewed chicken for the school when they aged and declined in egg production. The work of caring for the chickens was easy and pleasant and gave me a sense of accomplishment and belonging.

Often Monroe surprised me with a visit, coming by at first on the pretense that the feed bin needed filling and later on just to joke and flirt. One afternoon he surprised me with a first kiss. Perhaps he surprised himself as well, for it was spontaneous, catching me off guard, but filling me with pleasure. I went down to Farm House afterward, happy with the feeling of intimacy with Monroe.

The next morning as I went to feed the chickens and gather the eggs before breakfast, the huge rooster, who considered the flock of hens his exclusive property, rushed across the fenced yard and flew at me with his spurs outstretched. I was startled and angry and managed to kick the rooster viciously in self-defense. I did not relish the encounter, and at lunch I reported the attack to Georg, embellishing the account for emphasis and laughter.

That afternoon when I went again to feed and gather eggs, I was surprised to find the rooster hanging by his neck from the limb of a tree in the corner of the chicken yard. Instead of being shocked, I laughed heartily. It struck me as very funny. It was a great relief to know I would not encounter that rooster again. At supper that night, Georg told me in his mock serious manner that death was the price roosters had to pay for disturbing "pretty girls" who took care of his hens. Monroe had devised the punishment as one "fitting the crime," he said, but I knew Monroe had done it in fun, out of revenge, and in protection of me.

During the winter I also became better acquainted with the girls who finished the carvings in the shop. Jewell often brought crackers and peanut butter for a snack. When we took a break, she'd share with us, and eventually she asked us honestly to chip in on the expense. Her forthright honesty made her an excellent leader and set an example for industry and good nature. After we swept and cleaned up at three in the afternoon, she and I always walked together toward Keith House before going our separate ways. Jewell's friendly smile and honest answers to my many questions, coupled with her sense of responsibility and industriousness, gained my respect and made her my lifelong friend.

Another stalwart friend, Bea Massey, who worked with us in the shop, was one of the first people to really invite me to go home with her and spend the night. Her husband, Wallace, worked with Herman in the shop. They lived in Warne with Bea's mother, Mrs. Chambers, and Bea's unmarried sister. Mrs. Chambers was a widow and had a small house with a front porch looking out on U.S. Highway 64, not far from Shady Grove Church. Bea and Wallace were staying with her until they could get settled in a house of their own. Jewell and I both went home with them after work one afternoon.

Mrs. Chambers, a quick plump lady with graying brown hair confined in a bun at the back of her neck, welcomed us. Supper was ready. The table was set with bowls of soup beans, mashed Irish potatoes, fried chicken, biscuits, and gravy, still steaming in the pitcher. After supper, we all helped wash and dry the dishes and then visited together for a while before going to bed early.

As was the custom in many small mountain homes, the prized guest bed was in the front room. It was the most comfortable spot close to the "Warm Morning" wood heater. Jewell and I shared the high old-fashioned four-poster under patchwork quilts, piled high on top of a fluffy feather mattress. My enjoyment of that supper and breakfast the next morning went far beyond the nourishment and comfort I felt. It was so reassuring to experience acceptance into family life here that I felt as if I really belonged in the mountains.

During that year, Bea and Wallace moved to Brasstown and lived in one of the small rental houses. Mr. Bass Duval had built them to house workers who had come to the mountains to construct the TVA dams and powerhouses on the Hiwassee River. The houses were conveniently located close to the road across from the general store. Bea invited me often for Sunday dinner, and we continued our friendship as Bea and Wallace moved and their family grew.

Bea and Jewell were both important to me that winter. When I work or play and enjoy the companionship of achieving a common goal, the relationships that result are a source of great satisfaction. It was good to find these close friends among people in the mountains. Although life took us in different directions, I never lost the feeling of acceptance, understanding, and care that emanated from these first friends.

Louise Pitman also was a great companion and a friend. We especially worked well together. Soon after she came back from her two months up north, she, Mrs. Campbell, and I pitched in to do the early spring cleaning at Farm House. Every year the Board of Directors, a wonderful group from other parts of the country who had supported the Folk School since its founding, came to review its progress. In preparation for the inspection, every nook, cranny, window, and floor in every building was scoured and shined. No corner remained unexamined and unpolished. Every wooden wall was scrubbed, every barn wall and cellar whitewashed. The air of excitement was unequaled. Everything had to be in readiness. The spirit of camaraderie and anticipation built as we tried to outdo each other in preparing the homes and buildings.

In readying Farm House for inspection, shoulder-to-shoulder and elbow-to-elbow with Louise and Mrs. Campbell, I came to love them and the house as my own. In later years I would return to visit and stay there. I dearly loved the old rooms, the wide-board floors, the temperamental furnace, the quaint furniture, but it was, of course, Mrs. Campbell, who made it a home.

We woke up one morning to a heavy snowstorm—a beautiful excuse for a holiday. There were very few provisions for such unusual weather, so the roads were not plowed or salted. Snowcaps topped the fence posts, and wet snow clung to barbed wire along the road leading down to the barns from Farm House. All the usual work came to a halt, and an utter silence encompassed the land.

Louise and I took shovels, put on boots, and bundled up in sweaters, scarves, and jackets to walk down to Mill House. We wanted to see how Georg and Marguerite were surviving. The only telephone was at Keith House, so it was necessary to make personal visits to each house to be sure all was well.

The Bidstrups greeted us cheerfully, glad to have their isolation relieved. Marguerite offered us each an extra cup of coffee, and they shared their breakfast of Danish pastries with us before we moved on. Next, we waded knee-deep over the back trail and down to Pine View to check on the Carys before heading up the hill to Keith House. By that time the boys and Mr. Deschamps had the crucial paths dug, and everyone came out to build snowmen or engage in hilarious snowball fights.

The sun came out later that day, and by the next afternoon, only small patches of snow remained in shady spots on an occasional slope. However, the storm gave us all something to talk about for several weeks and united the Folk School family.

I began to feel an underlying sense of change, loss, and alienation despite the closeness I felt to those with whom I worked and played. Late in the winter, boys at the school and in the community began to enlist or be drafted into the army more rapidly. One afternoon Fred O. Scroggs came over to the shop to invite the students to a farewell party. His son, Boyd, had volunteered for service in the navy. Many of the country boys preferred that choice to the draft into the army. Service in the navy meant a clean bed and regular meals, in contrast to long marches and combat in muddy fields. Boyd was leaving soon for places unknown to any of us.

About that time, Harry Cary initiated the "Brasstown Blotter," a school newsletter to keep former students and men from the community in touch with each other and with home. Harry often enlisted my help in reporting for the "Blotter." Those who were serving our country in distant places always asked to be remembered here. The safe, self-sufficient world in the mountains was disappearing for many at the very time it beckoned to me. As the winter of 1941–42 passed, I realized that my year at the Folk School was nearing an end. With the coming of spring, I would need to make decisions about my future in this changing world.

Mountain Spring

"I loved to hear Georg tell about farming. He had just started a biodynamic garden experiment."

THE HILLS WERE GREENING. Each kind of tree was a different mound of soft spring verdancy. First, there were shades of pink on red maples, then the bright lime green of weeping willow trees appeared. Cone-shaped poplars dotted whole sides of mountains like sentinels, announcing the coming of April.

Each morning I walked from Farm House through the lumberyard to the shop. Boards stacked higher than my head lined both sides of the path. Above the wooden tunnel, the sky was a bright clear blue. The wood, washed with the showers of the previous evening, now steamed in the early sunlight. As I traveled betwixt the stacks, the wonderful subtle smell of newly cut lumber followed me. The mingled scents of pine, maple, apple, black walnut, and wild cherry promised things to come in the shapes of hand-hewn furniture and intricately carved menageries.

In the clearing where the woodworking shop sat surrounded by wild dogwood, snow white blooms shone bright against the deep sky. I stopped and looked back, engraving the experience in my memory. Instinctively, I knew that I would never again walk intimately through a lumberyard and catch that pungency without recalling this, my first spring at the Folk School.

Often after supper, a group gathered on the stone steps leading down from Keith House, comparing notes on the doings of the day and the plans for the future. The younger folk sat on the steps, the staff in the wooden Adirondack chairs on the lawn.

I loved to hear Georg tell about farming. He had just started a biodynamic garden experiment. I was interested in recycling organic material and in learning all I could about composting. I wanted to hear what he had planted that day and how the different crops were doing. Monroe often teased me by telling me some outrageous story about crops and then laughing when I asked a stupid question. Georg just smiled when I sympathized about the cows trampling down the rye field. He told me that it was heavy with ripe grain, ready to cut, and the wind, not the cows, had knocked it down. There was no real damage.

Georg was a patient teacher, loving to tell me seriously about farm life.

Marguerite liked to reminisce about her earlier years in Kentucky, where she rode her horse into remote areas from Pine Mountain Settlement School. One spring evening she was relatively quiet as she held a large scrapbook open on her lap. She and Georg were planning to move to their own property on the hills behind the creamery. One of Marguerite's classes with the girls was a planning class for homes. They clipped pictures of houses and furniture for their own scrapbooks, capturing their hopes and dreams for the future. Marguerite was formulating her own plans. We knew that sooner or later we would be able to see the rooms she was visualizing in such careful detail.

Miss Gaines sat quietly after a busy day planning meals and supervising their preparation. Gayle Isensee gave a clipped account of her excursions that day into the countryside. She had visited a young mother with a newborn baby, to help and to give advice about caring for the child. In the course of the afternoon, Gayle also looked into the health of the two older toddlers. She was full of admiration for the family and regretted that they had no electricity and no running water in the house.

"I don't see how these young mothers manage without modern conveniences. It will be good when we finally get electricity in this part of the country. I'm always surprised about how clean the babies are. The laundry is hanging in the sun, and the floors are clean swept," she said with a sigh.

Some of the students stayed on, having washed up the supper dishes and set the tables for breakfast. They whispered and giggled and occasionally chimed into the discussion with a question or observation. It was a quiet time after supper, full of peace and companionship.

One evening as we gathered there facing the mountains beyond Brasstown, fire encircled the top of one of the closer hills. In amazement I exclaimed, "Isn't that a beautiful sight! The outline of the fire in the dusk rings the top of the mountain. I've never seen anything quite like that!"

A chorus of objections rose to embarrass me with my ignorance of country things. "You don't want to say that, Ellie.

Forest fires are bad. People shouldn't be doing that."

"What is it? Who's doing it? And why, if it's so bad?"

"The old folks always used to burn off the woods in the spring to get rid of the bugs and the underbrush," Georg explained. "Now that there are so many settlements in this part of the country it's against the law."

"It's also dangerous. It can easily spread and catch fire to a house or barn, or burn someone's timber," Leila added.

"We'll get called to go and fight it if it comes closer to the school land," another student complained.

"It does make it easier to clear new ground, and new growth for grazing will turn that patch green," Georg added, "but it's not a good practice."

Burning of the woods in springtime was an old custom. As the land became settled, burning the woods was outlawed since it now endangered homes and forests. The practice was passing out of favor, but some rugged individuals persisted. Independence was still supreme in the mountains, and the Forest Service had to respond by calling out all hands to control the damage.

When the Folk School lands and those of our neighbors were in danger, the calls came, and all the students and staff turned out to clear firebreaks and to watch the lines. Sometimes backfires had to be set to burn toward the encroaching fire so that there would be nothing left in its path to ignite. Fighting fire with fire was necessary and acceptable.

That night the fire on Ghiringhelli Mountain, back of the Folk School, required a big crew from the school. Armed with rakes and shovels, we headed up the narrow wagon road that Frank Ghiringhelli had made to reach his small farm at the top of the mountain. After the Great Depression caused them to lose their dairy farm in Wisconsin, Mary and Frank heard of the Folk School's beginnings and were interested. They agreed to trade their farm machinery and some of their prize Jersey cows for a tract of land on top of Poor House Mountain above the school land. From then on, it was known locally as Ghiringhelli Mountain.

The forest trail branched off Frank's road, leading across the slope toward the river. There was a line of fire on the lower side of the path. We hove to and beat it out with rakes and hoes and brooms all along the line. Mr. Deschamps and Georg kept a sharp eye out for sparks igniting small drifts of leaves. Calmly they directed us one by one to stomp out each conflagration. We worked quickly. Luckily, the wind changed soon and blew toward the river, keeping the fire under control after we had extinguished it all along the spreading line.

Most of the Folk School gang was ready to go home when the crisis was over, but Mr. Deschamps asked for volunteers. Someone was needed to stay and watch, so that help could be summoned if it burned out of control again, or until rain extinguished all danger. He and Georg were delighted when Monroe and I assured them we would be glad to stay until all seemed safe. Amid friendly teasing, we settled down on a cleared flat spot where we could watch the dying line of fire further down the mountain.

"Wish I had brought some wieners," Monroe whispered. "I'm hungry. When I cook supper for myself at Tower House, I manage to have something that sticks to my ribs. Tonight the girls at Keith House went a little light on the soup beans and turnip greens."

"The corn bread, milk, and applesauce were all good," I observed, "but I'd like to toast some marshmallows. A good campfire always asks for a roast. They let us keep this little campfire until it dies down, but we need something to toast, and it looks like we're not going to have it. What have you been into today?"

"It's spring and time to clean out the lounging barn where the cows are kept, so you know good and well what I've been into," he laughed.

"You know what I meant. Any news from the community? I've been working all day and didn't even get to talk with Mrs. Green when I took the packages over to the post office this afternoon."

"Well, all I know is that Boyd Scroggs signed up for the navy, and Fred O. is going to give a big shindig going-away party next Saturday."

"That'll be fun. Don't you just love it here? There's always something going on."

"It's a good community, but sometimes I'm ready to see some other place. I'd go home to Hemptown if I could find a job there. I'll have to go into service anyway," he moaned.

"If you went off to Berea or the University of Georgia, you'd probably have time to finish college before they called you."

"No, if I'm called, I'm going. I'll not be a draft dodger. Anyway, Athens is too far and too snaky, and I don't have the money. I don't want to go to Berea. It's too much like the Folk School."

I laughed. He had a way of changing the subject. "You wouldn't want to leave the Folk School anyway," I said. "I think it's a great school. Even if I could probably make more money now somewhere else, I believe in what we're trying to do here, and I'm going to stick around for a while."

"I probably will too," he admitted, "but I'm really too young to settle down and probably need to see the world first."

Always as we shared experiences like this, we knew that despite the differences in our lives, we held many basic values in common. One of our disagreements usually came from the fact that Monroe said he was ready to explore other places, other jobs, while I still saw the Folk School as a cause that needed our full support. That night we didn't resolve the discussion because rain finally came to dampen our spirits and put the danger of fire to rest. With no further excuse for enjoying the evening, we headed home to our respective houses, parting at the kitchen door of Farm House.

Spring also brought my introduction to creek fishing. When the woods path leading from Keith House to Farm House burst into a glory of orange and yellow wild azalea, under-planted with a crowd of golden daffodils, Monroe persuaded me to go fishing in Little Brasstown Creek.

He had the cane poles, and he dug the worms. When it was suppertime, and he and the boys finished milking, I left Mrs. Campbell and Louise to have supper without me at Keith House, and I headed for the barn. They must have recognized the symptoms of true love, for otherwise I was never one to skip a good meal.

As I went through the big double doors at the front of the milking barn, the warm moist odor of steamy cows welcomed me. I walked the wide aisle between the back ends of the purebred Jersey cows. Fastened in stanchions with their names lettered in white chalk on black slates above their heads, they waited patiently to be released as they were milked one by one. Here and there, one was still attached to a milking machine.

Having observed and helped with the milking procedure many times, I made my way down among these cows, knowing most by name. Monroe was almost finished with his chores, so I did what I could to complete the work. Then we took a box of crackers, a quart of milk, and a can of Vienna sausages and headed past the blacksmith shop and the horse barn, down the gravel road that led to Little Brasstown Creek.

At the bridge we left the road and made our way downstream along the Little Brasstown Creek toward the Big Brasstown that came down the valley from Brasstown Bald, the highest mountain in Georgia. *Brasstown* was a mistranslation of the Indian word meaning "a place where the green grass grows." The community of Brasstown was located where Brasstown Creek met the Hiwassee River and considered itself also, "a place where the green grass grows."

Little Brasstown Creek curved through the fields, finding its way along strips of uncultivated pasture and past clean plowed fields recently planted in clover. The rich red-brown soil in one field was ready to be laid off in rows of corn. As the creek wandered through the fields, saplings and brush hung over it, and small pools of still water punctuated the flowing stream. Silently we stopped and baited our hooks with the fat red worms Monroe had dug from a corner of the barnyard. He carried them covered with moist dirt in a flat-sided Prince Albert tobacco can, which fit neatly in the back pocket of his jeans.

Hooks baited and thrown in, I perched on the bank and waited for a bite. Monroe worked his way a little further downstream, staying within earshot. It was hard to catch suckers because they just nibbled on the bait, but they were the most plentiful fish in the creek. They hardly ever took the whole worm, hook, line, and all, so it took patience to land one. Monroe said they were filled with tiny fine bones, so eating them was a chore. Still we were grateful for whatever we could get.

"Sometimes a catfish is resting on the bottom, just waiting for a juicy bite." Monroe told me. "A blue catfish makes good eating, but the yellow 'mud' cats are coarse in texture. They need to swim in fresh water for a spell before being eaten."

The first evening we fished together, a smallmouth bass made its way up the branch to surprise us. It put up a pretty good fight before Monroe landed it, gasping, on the bank. He was excited at the catch and bragged a bit. "I really like to catch bass. They're not easy. They give a good run for the money, but I'm pretty patient and usually manage to pull one in. Often I get red-eyed perch of varying sizes too, even here in the creek," he said.

Another evening I thought I'd made the catch of the year. There was a strong, persistent pull on the end of my line. I raised my cane pole up slowly, drawing the line in toward the bank. Quietly, lest I scare the fish into letting go, I called to Monroe. "Here's a big one!" I whispered hoarsely. He came back upstream and hovered behind me, directing me to keep steady as I braced myself on the narrow bank. With excitement equal to winning first prize at the fair, I pulled a heavy dead-weighted creature out on the muddy bank.

In triumph and confusion I asked, "What is it?"

"Just a mud dog," he said in disgust.

"But it looks like an alligator," I protested.

"Well they're related. It's a kind of salamander. The right name is mud puppy, but this one is big enough to be called a dog," he said, laughing. Taking out his pocketknife, he cut off its head and threw the body away. Then he cut the end of my line and threaded it with a fresh hook. "Now it won't sit there on the branch bottom, eating up little fish and fooling you into thinking you caught a big one," he concluded.

We worked our way companionably down Little Brasstown Creek to where it joined the Big Brasstown. Dusk gathered thickly. When we stood up and looked across the fields, we could see the lights on at Keith House. Reluctantly we headed in that direction, picking our way back through the woods at the edge of the field. Halfway between Keith House and Tower House, where Monroe lived, the little trail separated. He took the string of fish to cook on his fireplace for a solitary supper that night, although sometimes he tied the string of fish in the creek to keep them alive until he was ready to clean and cook them.

I took the woods path toward Farm House, noticing again a few wild daffodils that still hid in places where the sun seldom shone. It had been fun fishing with Monroe. He knew about many things that were new to me and had a great sense of humor and fun, but I enjoyed my time alone anticipating an evening with Louise and Mrs. Campbell. The peace of a full day of beauty and simple accomplishments went with me as I wondered if there was still time to work in the flower garden before nightfall.

Good-bye

Photo courtesy of the John C. Campbell Folk School Archives, Brasstown, North Carolina.

"It was difficult to say good-bye to my friends in Brasstown, to the mountains of Western North Carolina, to the Campbell Folk School . . ."

THEN IT WAS JUNE 1942. Flowers were blooming everywhere. Mrs. Campbell's flowerbed behind Farm House displayed a variety of lilies. Though the tulips had passed, the annuals were just beginning to bloom—zinnias, marigolds, and snapdragons against a hopeful background of dark green hollyhock spikes. Days were sunny, and by midday it was quite warm; nights were crisp and clear. I woke up at daylight to the repetitive repertoire of a persistent mockingbird perched on the power pole beside the kitchen window. Standing on tiptoe, I looked out my high windows to catch a glimpse of him and was rewarded by the sight of his small body, vibrating with the joy of song on the pole behind the flowerbed. Fog covered the ground with a foot-high, fluffy white blanket that would disappear as soon as the sun rose high above the mountains. The pungency of new-mown hay filled the air.

The regular term at the Folk School for mountain students was coming to a close. Many of the students would be returning home or to jobs elsewhere. A few young people who wanted to stay on at the school to work would be settling into their new jobs. At supper one night Georg said, "Tomorrow ve all go up on Wayah Bald to see the azaleas in bloom. Everyone who wants to see them better be ready right after breakfast. Miss Gaines and the girls vill pack us a picnic. While ve are a smaller family ve need to see the beauty around us."

As the fog began to lift, we caravanned over to Andrews. Then we continued up the narrow winding road to Aquone, where a tiny post office marked a crossroads community on the road toward Franklin. As we reached the gap of the mountain, where the road would begin the descent to the other side, we turned left onto a forest road leading upward on Wayah Bald. After a short drive on narrow gravel, we reached the area where azalea bushes, laden with huge white blossoms, lined both banks. In awe, we stopped chattering. I enjoyed the wild flame azaleas of early spring at the lower elevations, but the white ones with their lush growth and milky color were unexpectedly beautiful.

The top of the mountain was clear of tall trees. Mrs. Campbell told me at breakfast that day that no one seemed to know why the balds were bare, although a number of theories were offered. "Indian tribes used them for meeting places, gradually clearing them of wood for ceremonial fires. Early settlers who sought grazing for the animals they valued found these grassy tops a resource. Until they could clear fields from the dense woods around their homesteads, they took their stock to green pasture on the bald."

We drove out into the open bald, dotted and circled with more azaleas. There was a fire tower up there and a small observation patio for tourists. A thick low rock wall protected us from the steep mountain slope below. We had learned at Morning Song earlier that week that the men at the Civilian Conservation Corps camp nearby had built these during the years of the Great Depression. President Franklin Roosevelt had formed the CCC to provide work for the unemployed and to conserve our country's natural resources. Later, conscientious objectors, who refused to accept the draft into the army because of religious beliefs against war, had been assigned to the CCC. So, the work of conservation continued, and many wilderness areas were made accessible to us all.

We tumbled out of the car, overjoyed to stretch cramped legs. Below us, the valley encompassed undulating hills of green, punctuated with thickets of rhododendron and laurel. On the floor of this valley, winding roads all led toward Franklin, a distant cluster of stores, houses, and streets. For me the view was breathtaking, and I wanted to share my enthusiasm, but several of the students were very blasé about it. Having experienced mountain beauty all their lives, they were matter-of-fact in their appreciation.

Monroe had the day off from his job in the dairy and was able to go with us. I was glad because I knew that my time in Brasstown was ending. While Miss Gaines and the girls unpacked the lunch, he and I walked around the outer edge of the open bald, looking at some of the scattered azaleas in a variety of yellows and oranges.

"I'm glad you could come today, Muns," I confided. "You know I'm going to be leaving soon. I really hate to leave, but I need to go home at least for a while. You'll have to come see me."

"Yes, I'd like that. When I'm old enough to settle down, we could get married."

"When do you think that will be?" I asked, idly, having heard that refrain before and not wanting to pin him down to a date.

"I'll have to be in the military service," he replied. "I think I'll volunteer for the navy if my draft number looks close. I don't like the thought of fighting on the ground in all that mud and mess. At least on a ship, I'll have a place to put my stuff, a bunk, and regular meals. But I'll probably be killed overseas; I wouldn't want to leave you a widow." I laughed, and Monroe changed the subject abruptly.

He stooped down suddenly beside a tiny evergreen tree with shiny prickly leaves and bright red holly berries. "Look, Ellie, this is a small deciduous holly. It is like the other holly trees, but it sheds its leaves in winter, and they are just beginning to come back."

"You are really interested in bushes, plants, and herbs, aren't you?" I asked, disappointed at his abrupt change of subject. "You know so much about nature that you could teach me a lot. But why is it that you all aren't really interested in the distant mountains?"

"Well, I'll tell you," he conceded. "Most mountain people prefer the valleys, where we choose to build our homes closer to sources of water and accessible to roads. The mountains look down on us and are just a background for life. They are beautiful, but not worth so much 'oohing' and 'aahing.' "

We wandered back to the picnic area where Miss Gaines had unpacked our lunch and arranged it on the small stone table there. We sat on the wall or a bench nearby, eating stewed beef sandwiches on home-baked oatmeal bread with sweet bread-and-butter pickles. There was applesauce cake for dessert, and we washed it down with milk or iced tea. "What a great farewell party for the end of the regular school year!" I exclaimed enthusiastically as I thanked Miss Gaines and Georg for making it possible.

It had been a happy year for me. One evening later Georg privately assured me, "Ve hate to see you leave. I vill miss having you take care of the chickens, and I think you have grasped the Folk School vision more clearly than anyone else who has come for just a short time; I'm impressed with your way of adjusting to life in Brasstown and with your interest in farming. Ve'd like to see you stay."

Louise also urged me to stay. "Each staff member is entitled to a month's vacation away from the school with pay. Why don't you go home to Long Island for a vacation and come back for another school year here?" she asked.

It was tempting. I loved the school. It felt more like home than a workplace, but I would not be satisfied filling and packing orders for carvings much longer. Teaching here in crafts, music, dancing, or homemaking skills was not my calling. I didn't know what I could accomplish here that would be useful and satisfying.

All through the year, I had watched the role of the school in relation to the rest of the country. Many visitors came from different parts of the world. They drove to see the Folk School on the way to somewhere else. Some were educators, interested in noncompetitive styles of teaching or in the Scandinavian folk schools. Some had connections with the sprinkling of other experimental schools in this country, especially in Minnesota and Wisconsin. Other groups were simply curious travelers, eager to see the school and the crafts. Often they were families on the way to Florida for a winter vacation.

Frequently, I took my turn at Keith House on Sunday afternoon selling crafts from the gift shop, telling visitors about the school, or showing them around the property. I loved meeting people from other parts of the country, even fleetingly. They brought a perspective that relieved the isolation of this small enclave and gave me a sense that the folk school experiment could have an impact beyond our mountain community. It was a small salve for my itch to travel, and it gave me an opportunity to bounce my idealistic viewpoints off strangers.

I valued the philosophy of the school. I felt it offered an opportunity for a useful education to students for whom college was inaccessible and sometimes not even desired. Georg and I had many interesting conversations about the importance of education and the need for people to use what they learn in school to enrich their daily lives and the life of the community. The staff of the school encouraged former students who wanted to stay in Brasstown to build a community here by helping them purchase land and build houses. I liked that goal. I admired the frontier spirit of independence, ingenuity, and cooperation that was part of country and small-town life. It seemed to find its basis in concern for other people and in the ability to succeed in ways that didn't necessarily bring wealth or fame.

Many changes had occurred in the nine months since my arrival in Brasstown. More and more people had come into the area to build the TVA dams. Farmland had been flooded. Men and boys had been called into service. Girls and women found jobs in cities. The increased industry sparked by war was eliminating unemployment. The area still had the atmosphere of pioneer towns, and there was an exciting sense of opportunity. Temporary housing had been built for construction crews and flooded farmers. In Graham County, Fontana Village came into being, and Hiwassee Village grew around the dam in western Cherokee County. In Murphy, one movie theatre had grown to three. The A&P sold beer in a county that had been "dry."

The Folk School rented the upstairs and downstairs apartments in Hill House during the winter to two families of TVA engineers. I spent some time visiting there with a young mother from Yonkers, New York. I tried to cheer her by keeping her company in the loneliness she felt when her husband, whose work required long hours on the job, left her with no opportunity to get out and talk with other adults. She was grateful for my company because I had an aunt and uncle in Yonkers. Her culture shock was a reality check for me as I dimly recalled my homesick days in early September, when I first packed carvings to the tune of my own deep sighs. Now that seemed a long time ago, but the memory enabled me to really understand her feelings of isolation and nostalgia. I remembered the sense of alienation clearly.

Although I felt very much at home with the staff of the Folk School, I did not feel that I was contributing to the school program. I had virtually no contact with other people working widely in the region. Marguerite and Georg, Louise, and Mrs. Campbell were active in many contemporary area projects. Most of the staff were also. Together they were contributing far more to the mountain country than merely their work in Brasstown. Because the population was sparse, people maintained contact with others of similar interests despite the difficulties of distance and travel. This network encouraged the development of teaching programs for crafts, recreation, and farming.

Marguerite and Georg were particularly influential in the teaching of folk dancing in the mountains, and both brought a sophisticated taste of other cultures to the region. Louise was active in the development of high standards for crafts and their marketing, both in the mountains and beyond, particularly through the establishment of the Southern Highland Handicraft Guild in 1929, an association of artisans who needed to meet high standards of workmanship in order to become members. In 1942, there were two guild market shops, Allanstand in Asheville and another shop in Rockefeller Center in New York City.

Mrs. Campbell popularized the study of the history of the mountain area and catalogued her discovery of many of the ballads and folk songs that the early settlers brought with them from their Scots-Irish origins. Both she and Louise were craftswomen of distinction. Louise was an authority on vegetable dyes. Mrs. Campbell carved, and encouraged others to carve, unique animals and human figures. With regret, I could not identify any particular expertise of mine that would contribute in comparable ways.

With the coming of June, there was a new season at the school. It drew students from completely different backgrounds, seeking courses other than those of the regular Folk School program. Each year, the month of June brought "Short Courses." Teachers from other mountain schools came to share their experience and to enrich their repertoires of music, dance, and stories. There was dormitory space at the school now that most of the winter students had gone, and serious music and folklore enthusiasts came from New York, Boston, Washington, and other cities up north. Recreation, rather than daily living, became the focus of Folk School classes.

Recorder Week began the first week after our celebration on Wayah Bald. In preparation, everyone hustled and bustled to clean, cook, and collect teaching materials. In the shop, we filled and packed every back order on hand and spruced up the finishing room for visitors who might want to carve there in their free time. All the staff and students who played recorders brought them out and tuned them up. It was a new instrument for me, a small wooden flute with a whistle mouthpiece. It had become popular in England in the 1600s and was an appropriate accompaniment to the music, dance, and folk songs that were part of Folk School education.

Along with the preparations came the anticipation of special people arriving for the recorder and dance weeks. Excitement focused first on Philip Merrill, the musician who was coming from New York to teach recorder classes and to provide the music for two weeks of dancing.

One Friday night before the start of Recorder Week, Phil Merrill arrived. He was staying at Mill House, so he came to supper with the Folk School family and students. Afterward he played the piano and accordion for Friday Night dances. As we gathered in the living room before supper, Georg brought Phil over to introduce us.

"Ellie, this is Philip Merrill. He teaches music in New York City and is the musician for the Country Dance Society."

"Phil, this is Ellie Lambert. She has spent this year with us, but she is one of your fellow New Yorkers and a Vassar graduate."

We shook hands cordially. Phil was probably in his thirties and beginning to lose a bit of hair on top of his head, but he was slim and agile, dressed in jeans and a polo shirt. He had a broad New England accent and was a graduate of Julliard School of Music. Enthusiasm was second nature to Phil, and a marvelous smile lit up his face. Earlier in life, he had recovered from tuberculosis after lying flat on his back for a long stretch in a Saranac Lake, New York, sanitarium. If anyone had ever learned to value small pleasures through deprivation, it was Phil!

Meals with him were a delight. Georg's garden was producing bountifully, and the tables were loaded with fresh vegetables, deliciously cooked country-style in Miss Gaines's kitchen. There was fresh butter, hot bread, whole milk, and old-fashioned puddings. Phil savored every bite and always led the visitor chorus of admiring "oohs and aahs." He almost wrote a hymn of praise to the lowly cabbage, fresh from the garden.

Louise generously gave me time to attend classes, and she joined whenever she could find time. Each morning Mrs. Campbell taught the history of Appalachian music as it had been preserved from Scots-Irish music. Often she demonstrated with examples of songs and ballads, leading in her high clear soprano.

In the afternoons Phil and Mrs. Campbell taught recorder classes. One of the peak experiences in my life came at the end of my beginner course in soprano recorder with Phil. He rewarded each correct note any of his students played with smiles and nods. We practiced "Drink to Me Only with Thine Eyes" repeatedly until, at the recital in conclusion of the week, even I could stay with the group. It was an experience of total success for me, much like hitting a perfect drive in golf, one you never forget!

Dance Week followed Recorder Week, and a new influx of people came from the "settlement" schools in Kentucky, southern Virginia, Tennessee, and the entire mountain area. Jean and Edna Ritchie, sisters to Mae Deschamps, who lived here at the school in Rock House, came from Kentucky to sing and teach new dances. There were several Ritchie sisters from the mountains of eastern Kentucky, and they had an inherited store of ballads to sing and stories to tell. All were skilled dancers as well.

May Gadd, head of the Country Dance Society in New York, came to teach new dances and old. She was pretty, plump, middle-aged, and a talented dancer. Her country dresses with full skirts and tight bodices were beautiful, probably products of an expert seamstress or a fashionable New York department store. Marguerite's dresses ran close competition. All the women wore full-skirted country dresses, in calico and gingham. It was a colorful time, and I felt a bit shabby in the broomstick flowered print skirt that had been my standby for a year.

The community was welcome to come for the evening classes and to some morning classes as well. I had the whole week off to participate. The spirit of the school changed with the arrival of these students for short courses. During the regular school year, roles were simple and life uncomplicated. This innocence and simplicity disappeared with the advent of these people who were at home in many different environments. With the scarcity of student workers, I was pushed into service. In the afternoon, I was in charge of transporting and serving cookies at each of the different houses. These teas seemed unnecessary to me, somewhat troublesome, and artificial, as though we were trying to impress visitors. I much preferred my customary chicken-feeding responsibilities.

I was glad that early in June I had decided to go back up north for a year at least. I felt I had learned all I had hoped for the previous September when I had begun my search to see more of the world beyond the Hudson River. I had found friendly accepting friends and neighbors, and stimulating teachers, whose work I admired. I loved feeding chickens, milking cows, gardening, and experiencing a simple way of life.

The vision of a community continuing to learn, work, and play together was exciting to me. Monroe and I had a good friendship that might result in marriage, but neither of us was certain of that. He, like the rest of the men, would leave soon for the war. I would miss all that I had come to love here, but I needed to see more of the world before I could settle down.

I was curious to discover how the rest of the country was responding to the war. I was eager to find work that would satisfy me intellectually and fulfill the need for meaning in my life. I wanted to earn some money and buy a farm. The study of rural sociology at Columbia University or graduate study in teaching beckoned me. There were many choices ahead, and I was ambivalent about them all.

I needed to go home again and rethink the future. It was difficult to say good-bye to my friends in Brasstown, to the mountains of Western North Carolina, to the Campbell Folk School, but the idea of enriching, enlivening, and enlightening country living were deeply planted in my soul.

Mrs. Campbell offered to let Monroe drive me to Asheville to catch the train to New York. We talked all the way. Then on the small open platform of the Southern Railway station in Asheville, self-conscious of other people around us, we embraced and kissed each other good-bye in the polite, reticent fashion of the time. I watched Monroe and waved to him from the window of the train until we moved out of sight.

My return trip back north was more direct than my wandering journey to Brasstown had been the previous September. From Asheville I rode on the jolting day coach, my eyes glued to the dusty window as the mountains slipped away. In Salisbury, North Carolina, we had to change trains. I waited there in the dark on the platform with little groups of other travelers, wondering what would come next into my life.

When the express train rushed into the station, I scrambled with my suitcases, boxes, coats, and other miscellaneous packages up the steep steps to the platform between cars. With several fellow travelers pressing behind me, I found that every seat in the car ahead was taken. Soldiers and sailors in uniform filled the aisle. Some were groggy with sleep, others cheerful, friendly, filled with good spirit.

This was a different, exciting world. I wondered if I would find a place in it again. One young sailor rose from a corner seat near the door and motioned me to take his place. Exhausted and grateful, I sank into it. The train gathered speed and rushed me north through the dark night, away from the mountains I loved. Almost at once, I knew I would return.

Ellie's Photo Album

The photographs that make up Ellie's photo album are from a number of sources. Most were taken by Ellie herself. In the instance where she had no picture of an important person, place, or thing, the Folk School archives were scoured to fill in the gaps even if the time period wasn't quite perfect.

This was the "big house" at Saint Timothy's School in Catonsville, Maryland. Ann and I spent three years there before attending Vassar. In college we regaled our friends with stories of the discipline we had experienced and the fun we had. We wanted to show Liz and Peg these quaint and wonderful halls, so we spent the first night of our southern tour there.

Postcard published by the Meriden Gravure Company
Meriden, Connecticut

As we traveled the second day, we saw the restoration of the colonial village at Williamsburg, Virginia, which was in progress. My friends admired the architecture, and I noted contrast between new and old as I snapped a picture of the Powder Magazine.

On Tybee Island in Savannah we threw off our shoes and socks and danced joyfully. Liz Foote, Peg Greene, and Ann Nash posed for me. Aren't they gorgeous? Didn't we have fun?

The landscape surrounding Copper Hill, Tennessee, was barren. The red-clay hills were naked of vegetation as far as eyes could see. Trees, grass, and flowers had been ravaged by the sulfuric acid fumes emitted from the copper smelters. I bought this postcard to mail home to verify the devastation.

When we reached South Carolina, we stood shoe-deep in sticky red clay at the construction site of the Santee-Cooper Dam. A guard explained the accelerated plan for the huge earthen dam that would provide flood control and an electric power plant. I stood with Peg, the guard, and Liz as Ann took our picture. We were fascinated with the engineering information.

Ann Nash

Louise Lambert

My sister took this picture of me and her tiny cocker puppy on the steps of our cottage in Pemaquid Point, Maine. It was my last vacation before going to work at the John C. Campbell Folk School in North Carolina.

The entrance to Keith House, the center of community life at the Folk School. My first home at the school was on the second floor.

Marguerite Butler co-founded the Folk School with Olive Campbell. In 1936, she married Georg Bidstrup. Here she is on the path to Little Brasstown Baptist Church, where she some-times taught an adult class.

Georg Bidstrup in front of the dairy barn silo. When Mrs. Campbell and Marguerite Butler toured the Scandinavian folk schools, they met Georg and invited him to come to Brasstown to teach farming and manage the farm. He and Marguerite taught folk dancing for the Friday Night Games.

This photograph from a Folk School brochure shows Olive Dame Campbell carving with a chisel and mallet. I often watched her carve during my year at the school.

Louise Pitman was the head of the Crafts Department at the Folk School in 1941. She was my "boss" and good friend. She specialized in making vegetable dyes and was later the head of the Southern Highland Handicraft Guild. I lived with Louise and Mrs. Campbell at Farm House, and we went in and out of this kitchen door.

Monroe reading the paper on the front terrace of Keith House. Was he ever proud of those boots! Monroe was a Folk School student who stayed on to manage the school dairy herd.

Herman Estes and Wallace Massey in front of the woodworking shop. Herman was in charge of the shop and Wallace helped him.

Monroe Wilson and Jewell Sales clowning in front of the woodworking shop. Monroe was in charge of the dairy, and Jewell worked in the finishing room. She has my "Southwester" on to impersonate me!

Monroe (wearing the hat) always provided a laugh for the finishing team: Annie Laurie, Peavine, Jewell, and Bea.

The back door of the wood-working shop, through which I often entered to begin my day of packing carvings to be sent to faraway shops.

These are examples of typical Folk School carvings, usually farm animals and local wildlife.

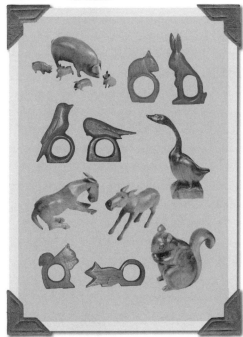

Photo courtesy of the John C. Campbell Folk School Archives, Brasstown, North Carolina.

This table in the woodworking shop is filled with carvings awaiting their finishing coat.

The first time I visited Harriet and Gwen Cornwell's new house, it was not yet finished, but Gwen pointed out what was planned for each area of the farm.

Herman and Mabel Estes lived and worked at the Folk School. Their three children, Dick, Helen, and Doodle, became my fond friends.

An early picture of the grocery store of the Mountain Valley Cooperative in Brasstown. At the creamery further east on the highway, the co-op processed dairy and poultry products from small farms in the area.

I took orders to be shipped and picked up the mail here at the Brasstown post office.

The "loafers' bench" in Fred O. Scroggs's General Store inspired Mrs. Campbell to teach carving. She had a copy of this picture in her office.

Daisy Dame. Photo courtesy of the John C. Campbell Folk School Archives, Brasstown, North Carolina.

Granny Scroggs showing off her Christmas cactus. The Scroggs family had donated land for the establishment of the Folk School.

One half of Mill House served as the boys' dormitory and the other half as a residence for the Bidstrups. It also functioned as a working water pump for the reservoir on the hill above the Folk School.

Wayne and Gladys Holland in front of Mill House, where they were married. Wayne worked at the Mountain Valley Cooperative, and Gladys was Miss Gaines's assistant at the Folk School.

June and Harry Cary worked as volunteers at the Folk School, 1940–42. June is a niece of Mrs. Campbell, and Harry grew up in a missionary family in Japan.

This is Tower House, where Monroe lived at the Folk School. He and I spent many hours walking the path between Tower House and Farm House, where I lived.

The crowd gathered outside each Sunday at Little Brasstown Baptist Church. Most people walked to the church, and services were a center of social life in the community.

The young people's class at Little Brasstown Baptist Church. They taught me a great deal about my own religious beliefs as I strove to understand theirs. We sat on a log or on the ground under the trees in front of the church.

Everyone at the Folk School helped with the chores. This is the chicken house where I fed the chickens and gathered the eggs.

Georg Bidstrup's faithful dog, Jack, waits on the Campbell Trail.

My view of Farm House and the garage when returning from the chicken house.

The Folk School dairy barns. The barn at the left was the milking barn, and the one on the right was the lounging barn, where the cows were housed during inclement weather.

This is the road leading down from Farm House to the barns. During a storm in the winter of 1942, the unusually heavy snowstorm blanketed the area and isolated the school for two days.

Gene and Bump. When the boys cut firewood for all the Folk School houses, Georg took time to teach them how to stack it in a rounded cone in the traditional Danish way.

Monroe took me to the Cherokee County Fair—my first date in the mountains. As the school year progressed, he and I became the best of friends.

Here I am sitting on the fence in front of Tower House, waiting to go fishing with Monroe in the Little Brasstown Creek.

Monroe Wilson

While waiting for dinner, Monroe and I worked the crossword puzzles at this game table in Keith House.

Beautiful furniture and carvings were created from the pine, cherry, walnut, and maple boards cut here in the sawmill and stored in the wood sheds.

I often took this path through the lumberyard on the way from Keith House to the woodworking shop. I loved the pungent odor of freshly cut wood.

Here, Oscar Cantrell and Monroe work in the blacksmith's shop. Oscar was the farm foreman and blacksmith. He taught basic smithing skills as well as decorative techniques.

This is the path that we took from Keith House to the woodworking shop, where I worked packing carvings for shipment.

Mrs. Campbell, seated in the Adirondack chair, often held classes and informal discussions outside.

Dub Martin and Monroe carrying water from Farm House to an outside gathering. Everyone helped to make life comfortable for our "short course" visitors.

Farm House was where I lived with Mrs. Campbell and Louise Pitman. It became "home" to me at the Folk School.

Mrs. Campbell loved gardening, and I often helped her work in her large garden at Farm House.

This was the view of the mountains from the front of Farm House. It was one of my favorite Brasstown scenes.

Our wedding day.

Epilogue

MONROE AND I WERE MARRIED on October 18, 1945, at my home in Cedarhurst, Long Island, New York. In December, after holidays with my family, we drove my newly acquired 1935 Ford sedan with all our worldly possessions to Georgia. We stayed there with Monroe's mother until we returned to jobs at the Folk School after the first of the year.

In our free time at the school, we built much of our own furniture. I wove runners and placemats for the Folk School and for myself. We also had a large vegetable garden. In 1948–49, I taught seventh grade at Martin's Creek School, and we decided to settle in Brasstown. We bought the farm of Harriet and Gwen Cornwell that I had first visited as their home was being built in 1941.

Our four children were born and reared in that home. Monroe became the postmaster in Brasstown. After the children were in school, I became a social worker and then a family counselor. We modeled our home on many of the ideals of the Folk School, built furniture, and grew most of our food.

We often participated in Folk School activities and sometimes helped to shape changes there. It has been a source of great pleasure to see the school and the community grow and change while retaining many of the goals for which the school was founded, enriching the life of this beautiful Southern Appalachian community.

About the Author

Virginia Porter Reynolds

ELEANOR LAMBERT GREW UP on Long Island and graduated from Vassar College in 1941. Her sense of adventure led her to leave the conventional society of her youth to take a job at the John C. Campbell Folk School in the tiny Appalachian community of Brasstown. After World War II, Ellie married Monroe Wilson, with whom she had fallen in love at the Folk School, and in 1949, the Wilsons bought a dairy farm in Brasstown. During their marriage of over fifty years, they reared four children: Danny, Anne, John, and Florence.

Ellie honed her listening and writing skills while employed as a teacher, social worker, and psychiatric counselor. She received a master's degree in nonschool counseling in 1979. Her spirit of advocacy led to her involvement in establishing several community service agencies. In 1955, she and Monroe were founding members of Hayesville's Episcopal Church of the Good Shepherd. Ellie's enduring sense of wonder and love of God make her a joyful student of the Bible.

Now semiretired, she lists among her hobbies "learning new skills and appreciating them in others," no doubt an indispensable quality for a grandmother of six. Ellie attributes her love of people and of life to having interacted with a wide variety of people through her many activities in Western North Carolina.

Publisher's Note

PHOTOGRAPHS IN THIS BOOK which bear no credit line were taken by the author or are from her collection. Photos from other sources are credited and the photographer, if known, is named. Each chapter of *My Journey to Appalachia* is preceded by a photograph; these beautiful images are the property of the John C. Campbell Folk School, who generously allowed their use to illustrate this work. Most of the images were taken by the renowned photographer Doris Ulmann; several by photographers unknown to us; and one by Olive Dame Campbell's sister, Daisy. Though the portraits date from nearly a decade before Eleanor Lambert arrived at the Folk School, they so richly capture the spirit and character of the individuals that their inclusion in this book was thought appropriate.

Doris Ulmann (1882–1934) was a wealthy New York pictorialist photographer who began her work as a studio portrait photographer. She photographed many of the famous and elite individuals of her day. In the late 1920s, her interest turned from studio work to the field. It was her desire to record the lives and work of vanishing "American types," among these the people of Appalachia. After being injured in a fall, Ulmann found it difficult to work in the field with her cumbersome equipment, so she hired the folk song collector and performer John Jacob Niles as her assistant. His prior contacts facilitated Ulmann's introduction to the people of the region.

Ulmann's work is firmly grounded in the pictorialist school of photography, a style that seeks to elevate the discipline above mere documentation to that of fine art on par with painting. The pictorialist relied heavily on his control of composition, light, and expression to create an image that would convey to the viewer an entire story. Ulmann treated the Appalachian people with the same degree of respect as she treated her rich and powerful New York clients, and she wanted her subjects to be themselves, often posing them in their everyday attire with the tools or end products of their trade or craft. Ulmann generally took her photographs with a view camera without a shutter, using glass-plate negatives. The soft-focus style of her work gives an impressionistic quality to her images.

Doris Ulmann had experimented with various types of developing during her career: bromoil, oil pigment, gum bichromate, platinum, and gelatin silver printing. The process she used most frequently was the costly platinum print. This form of printing offers the photographer a wide range of tone and a soft texture unlike any other process. It also creates one of the most stable and enduring prints.

In 1933, Ulmann was approached by Allen Eaton, who was working on *Handicrafts of the Southern Highlands*, to provide photographs for his book. Eaton arranged for her to visit the John C. Campbell Folk School, an opportunity Ulmann seized with enthusiasm, knowing Olive Campbell's work there. In early July 1933, Ulmann and Niles left for North Carolina. During her few weeks there, Ulmann photographed individuals from the school and the surrounding countryside. Though Ulmann sought to record a vanishing way of life in Appalachia, her work transcends the documentary style of photography.

Ulmann and Niles returned to the Folk School in December of 1933 at the invitation of Mrs. Campbell to join the school in its holiday festivities. Ulmann had formed a fast friendship with Mrs. Campbell and loved the school dearly. She again returned in April and June of 1934. There she continued to photograph the activities of the school and the people of the area. Ellie says,"When I arrived at the school in 1941, there was still much excitement about Miss Ulmann's visit," and she remembers many of the Ulmann portraits "displayed prominently . . . over the years." Doris Ulmann became ill during the summer of 1934 and died on August 28 at her home in New York. At the time of her death, Ulmann had thousands of undeveloped glass-plate negatives. These plates were developed posthumously by photographer Samuel Lifshey, using the gelatin silver printing process (basic black-and-white processing).

Doris Ulmann left the John C. Campbell Folk School a generous monetary bequest as well as her collection of Folk School images. Perhaps of equal value to posterity, these images provide a record not only of the faces who made up the Folk School, but of the spirit that founded it and can still be felt there today.

Bright Mountain Books would like to thank David A. Brose, John C. Campbell Folk School Folklorist, for his time and assistance in combing though the school's pictorial archives.

Chapter opening photographs are as follows:

Bibliography

Eaton, Allen H. *Handicrafts of the Southern Highlands*. New York: Dover, 1973.

Jacobs, Philip Walker. *The Life and Photography of Doris Ulmann*. Lexington, KY: University Press of Kentucky, 2001.

Naef, Weston, ed. 1996. *Doris Ulmann: Photographs from the J. Paul Getty Museum*. In Focus. Malibu: The J. Paul Getty Museum.